FORWARD/COMMENTARY

The National Institute of Standards and Technology (NIST) is a measurement standards laboratory, and a non-regulatory agency of the **United States Department of Commerce**. Its mission is to promote innovation and industrial competitiveness. Founded in 1901, as the National Bureau of Standards, NIST was formed with the mandate to provide standard weights and measures, and to serve as the national physical laboratory for the United States. **With a** world-class measurement and testing laboratory encompassing a wide range of areas of computer science, mathematics, statistics, and systems engineering, NIST's cybersecurity program supports its overall mission to promote U.S. innovation and industrial competitiveness by advancing measurement science, standards, and related technology through research and development in ways that enhance economic security and improve our quality of life.

The need for cybersecurity standards and best practices that address interoperability, usability and privacy has been shown to be critical for the nation. NIST's cybersecurity programs seek to enable greater development and application of practical, innovative security technologies and methodologies that enhance the country's ability to address current and future computer and information security challenges.

The cybersecurity publications produced by NIST cover a wide range of cybersecurity concepts that are carefully designed to work together to produce a holistic approach to cybersecurity primarily for government agencies and constitute the best practices used by industry. This holistic strategy to cybersecurity covers the gamut of security subjects from development of secure encryption standards for communication and storage of information while at rest to how best to recover from a cyber-attack.

Why buy a book you can download for free? We print this so you don't have to.

Some are available only in electronic media. Some online docs are missing pages or barely legible.

We at 4th Watch Publishing are former government employees, so we know how government employees actually use the standards. When a new standard is released, an engineer prints it out, punches holes and puts it in a 3-ring binder. While this is not a big deal for a 5 or 10-page document, many NIST documents are over 100 pages and printing a large document is a time consuming effort. So, an engineer that's paid $75 an hour is spending hours simply printing out the tools needed to do the job. That's time that could be better spent doing engineering. We publish these documents so engineers can focus on what they were hired to do – engineering. It's much more cost-effective to just order the latest version from Amazon.com

If there is a standard you would like published, let us know. Our web site is
www.usgovpub.com

Many of our titles are available as ePubs for Kindle, iPad, Nook, remarkable, BOOX, and Sony eReaders. Please visit our web site to see our recommendations.

Why buy an eBook when you can access data on a website for free? HYPERLINKS

Yes, many books are available as a PDF, but not all PDFs are bookmarked? Do you really want to search a 6,500-page PDF document manually? Load our copy onto your Kindle, PC, iPad, Android Tablet, Nook, or iPhone (download the FREE kindle App from the APP Store) and you have an easily searchable copy. Most devices will allow you to easily navigate an ePub to any Chapter. Note that there is a distinction between a Table of Contents and "Page Navigation". Page Navigation refers to a different sort of Table of Contents. Not one appearing as a page in the book, but one that shows up on the device itself when the reader accesses the navigation feature. Readers can click on a navigation link to jump to a Chapter or Subchapter. Once there, most devices allow you to "pinch and zoom" in or out to easily read the text. (Unfortunately, downloading the free sample file at Amazon.com does not include this feature. You have to buy a copy to get that functionality, but as inexpensive as eBooks are, it's worth it.) Kindle allows you to do word search and Page Flip (temporary place holder takes you back when you want to go back and check something). Visit **www.usgovpub.com** to learn more.

1
2

**DRAFT (2nd) NIST Special Publication 800-52
Revision 2**

3
4
5

Guidelines for the Selection, Configuration, and Use of Transport Layer Security (TLS) Implementations

6

7
8
9

Kerry McKay
David Cooper

10

11

12

13

14

15

C O M P U T E R   S E C U R I T Y

16

17

DRAFT (2nd) NIST Special Publication 800-52
Revision 2

Guidelines for the Selection, Configuration, and Use of Transport Layer Security (TLS) Implementations

Kerry McKay
David Cooper
Computer Security Division
Information Technology Laboratory

October 2018

U.S. Department of Commerce
Wilbur L. Ross, Jr., Secretary

National Institute of Standards and Technology
Walter Copan, NIST Director and Under Secretary of Commerce for Standards and Technology

49 **Authority**

50 This publication has been developed by NIST in accordance with its statutory responsibilities under the
51 Federal Information Security Modernization Act (FISMA) of 2014, 44 U.S.C. § 3551 *et seq.*, Public Law
52 (P.L.) 113-283. NIST is responsible for developing information security standards and guidelines, including
53 minimum requirements for federal information systems, but such standards and guidelines shall not apply
54 to national security systems without the express approval of appropriate federal officials exercising policy
55 authority over such systems. This guideline is consistent with the requirements of the Office of Management
56 and Budget (OMB) Circular A-130.

57 Nothing in this publication should be taken to contradict the standards and guidelines made mandatory and
58 binding on federal agencies by the Secretary of Commerce under statutory authority. Nor should these
59 guidelines be interpreted as altering or superseding the existing authorities of the Secretary of Commerce,
60 Director of the OMB, or any other federal official. This publication may be used by nongovernmental
61 organizations on a voluntary basis and is not subject to copyright in the United States. Attribution would,
62 however, be appreciated by NIST.

63 National Institute of Standards and Technology Special Publication 800-52 Revision 2
64 Natl. Inst. Stand. Technol. Spec. Publ. 800-52 Rev. 2, 71 pages (October 2018)
65 CODEN: NSPUE2

66 Certain commercial entities, equipment, or materials may be identified in this document in order to describe an
67 experimental procedure or concept adequately. Such identification is not intended to imply recommendation or
68 endorsement by NIST, nor is it intended to imply that the entities, materials, or equipment are necessarily the best
69 available for the purpose.

70 There may be references in this publication to other publications currently under development by NIST in accordance
71 with its assigned statutory responsibilities. The information in this publication, including concepts and methodologies,
72 may be used by federal agencies even before the completion of such companion publications. Thus, until each
73 publication is completed, current requirements, guidelines, and procedures, where they exist, remain operative. For
74 planning and transition purposes, federal agencies may wish to closely follow the development of these new
75 publications by NIST.

76 Organizations are encouraged to review all draft publications during public comment periods and provide feedback to
77 NIST. Many NIST cybersecurity publications, other than the ones noted above, are available at
78 https://csrc.nist.gov/publications.

79

80 **Public comment period: *October 15, 2018* through *November 16, 2018***

81 National Institute of Standards and Technology
82 Attn: Computer Security Division, Information Technology Laboratory
83 100 Bureau Drive (Mail Stop 8930) Gaithersburg, MD 20899-8930
84 Email: sp80052-comments@nist.gov

85 All comments are subject to release under the Freedom of Information Act (FOIA).

Reports on Computer Systems Technology

The Information Technology Laboratory (ITL) at the National Institute of Standards and Technology (NIST) promotes the U.S. economy and public welfare by providing technical leadership for the Nation's measurement and standards infrastructure. ITL develops tests, test methods, reference data, proof of concept implementations, and technical analyses to advance the development and productive use of information technology. ITL's responsibilities include the development of management, administrative, technical, and physical standards and guidelines for the cost-effective security and privacy of other than national security-related information in federal information systems. The Special Publication 800-series reports on ITL's research, guidelines, and outreach efforts in information system security, and its collaborative activities with industry, government, and academic organizations.

Abstract

Transport Layer Security (TLS) provides mechanisms to protect data during electronic dissemination across the Internet. This Special Publication provides guidance to the selection and configuration of TLS protocol implementations while making effective use of Federal Information Processing Standards (FIPS) and NIST-recommended cryptographic algorithms. It requires that TLS 1.2 configured with FIPS-based cipher suites be supported by all government TLS servers and clients and requires support of TLS 1.3 by January 1, 2024. This Special Publication also provides guidance on certificates and TLS extensions that impact security.

Keywords

information security; network security; SSL; TLS; Transport Layer Security

Acknowledgements

The authors, Kerry McKay and David Cooper of the National Institute of Standards and Technology (NIST), would like to thank the many people who assisted with the development of this document. In particular, we would like to acknowledge Tim Polk of NIST and Santosh Chokhani of CygnaCom Solutions, who were co-authors on the first revision of this document. We would also like to acknowledge Matthew J. Fanto and C. Michael Chernick of NIST and Charles Edington III and Rob Rosenthal of Booz Allen and Hamilton who wrote the initial published version of this document.

Audience

This document assumes that the reader of these guidelines is familiar with TLS protocols and public-key infrastructure concepts, including, for example, X.509 certificates.

122	**Note to Reviewers**

123 The Triple Data Encryption Algorithm (TDEA), also known as 3DES, is no longer approved for
124 use with TLS (see Department of Homeland Security Binding Operational Directive BOD-18-01,
125 https://cyber.dhs.gov/assets/report/bod-18-01.pdf). The 64-bit block size does not provide
126 adequate protection in applications such as TLS where large amounts of data are encrypted under
127 the same key.

128 This draft also requires agencies to add support for TLS 1.3 by January 1, 2024. TLS 1.3 and 1.2
129 are intended to coexist, and support for both is encouraged after the TLS 1.3 adoption deadline.

130 **Executive Summary**

131   Office of Management and Budget (OMB) Circular A-130, *Managing Information as a Strategic*
132   *Resource,* requires managers of public-facing information repositories or dissemination systems
133   that contain sensitive but unclassified data to ensure that sensitive data is protected
134   commensurate with the risk and magnitude of the harm that would result from the loss, misuse,
135   or unauthorized access to or modification of such data. Given the nature of interconnected
136   networks and the use of the Internet to share information, the protection of this sensitive data can
137   become difficult if proper mechanisms are not employed to protect the data. Transport Layer
138   Security (TLS) provides such a mechanism to protect sensitive data during electronic
139   dissemination across the Internet.

140   TLS is a protocol created to provide authentication, confidentiality, and data integrity protection
141   between two communicating applications. TLS is based on a precursor protocol called the Secure
142   Sockets Layer Version 3.0 (SSL 3.0) and is considered to be an improvement to SSL 3.0. SSL
143   3.0 is specified in [31]. The Transport Layer Security version 1 (TLS 1.0) specification is an
144   Internet Request for Comments, RFC 2246 [22]. Each document specifies a similar protocol that
145   provides security services over the Internet. TLS 1.0 has been revised to version 1.1, as
146   documented in RFC 4346 [23], and TLS 1.1 has been further revised to version 1.2, as
147   documented in RFC 5246 [24]. In addition, some extensions have been defined to mitigate some
148   of the known security vulnerabilities in implementations using TLS versions 1.0, 1.1, and 1.2.
149   TLS 1.3, described in RFC 8446 [50], is a significant update to previous versions that includes
150   protections against security concerns that arose in previous versions of TLS.

151   This Special Publication provides guidance to the selection and configuration of TLS protocol
152   implementations while making effective use of NIST-approved cryptographic schemes and
153   algorithms. In particular, it requires that TLS 1.2 be configured with cipher suites using NIST-
154   approved schemes and algorithms as the minimum appropriate secure transport protocol and
155   requires support for TLS 1.3 by January 1, 2024.[1] When interoperability with non-government
156   systems is required, TLS 1.1 and TLS 1.0 may be supported. This Special Publication also
157   identifies TLS extensions for which mandatory support must be provided and other
158   recommended extensions.

159   The use of the recommendations provided in this Special Publication would promote:

160   • More consistent use of authentication, confidentiality and integrity mechanisms for the
161   protection of information transported across the Internet;

162   • Consistent use of the recommended cipher suites that encompass NIST-approved
163   algorithms and open standards;

164   • Protection against known and anticipated attacks on the TLS protocol; and

---

[1] While SSL 3.0 is the most secure of the SSL protocol versions, it is not approved for use in the protection of Federal
  information because it relies in part on the use of cryptographic algorithms that are not NIST-approved. TLS 1.2 is approved
  for the protection of Federal information when properly configured. TLS versions 1.1 and 1.0 are approved only when they are
  required for interoperability with non-government systems and are configured according to these guidelines.

165   • Informed decisions by system administrators and managers in the integration of TLS
166   implementations.

167   While these guidelines are primarily designed for Federal users and system administrators to
168   adequately protect sensitive but unclassified U.S. Federal Government data against serious
169   threats on the Internet, they may also be used within closed network environments to segregate
170   data. (The client-server model and security services discussed also apply in these situations).
171   This Special Publication supersedes NIST Special Publication 800-52 Revision 1. This Special
172   Publication should be used in conjunction with existing policies and procedures.

173

174
175   **Table of Contents**

251

1   Introduction

253   Transport Layer Security (TLS) protocols are used to secure communications in a wide variety of
254   online transactions such as financial transactions (e.g., banking, trading stocks, e-commerce),
255   healthcare transactions (e.g., viewing medical records or scheduling medical appointments), and
256   social transactions (e.g., email or social networking). Any network service that handles sensitive
257   or valuable data, whether it is personally identifiable information (PII), financial data, or login
258   information, needs to adequately protect that data. TLS provides a protected channel for sending
259   data between the server and the client. The client is often, but not always, a web browser.
260   Memorandum M-15-13[2] requires that all publicly accessible Federal websites and web services
261   only provide service through a secure connection.[3] The initiative to secure connections will
262   enhance privacy and prevent modification of the data from government sites in transit.

263   TLS is a layered protocol that runs on top of a reliable transport protocol – typically the
264   Transmission Control Protocol (TCP). Application protocols, such as the Hypertext Transfer
265   Protocol (HTTP) and the Internet Message Access Protocol (IMAP), can run above TLS. TLS is
266   application independent, and used to provide security to any two communicating applications
267   that transmit data over a network via an application protocol.

268   ## 1.1   History of TLS

269   The SSL protocol was designed by the Netscape Corporation to meet security needs of client and
270   server applications. Version 1 of SSL was never released. SSL 2.0 was released in 1995, but had
271   well-known security vulnerabilities, which were addressed by the 1996 release of SSL 3.0.
272   During this timeframe, the Microsoft Corporation released a protocol known as Private
273   Communications Technology (PCT), and later released a higher performance protocol known as
274   the Secure Transport Layer Protocol (STLP). PCT and STLP never commanded the market share
275   that SSL 2.0 and SSL 3.0 commanded. The Internet Engineering Task Force (IETF), a technical
276   working group responsible for developing Internet standards to ensure communications
277   compatibility across different implementations, attempted to resolve security engineering and
278   protocol incompatibility issues between the protocols as best it could. The IETF standards track
279   Transport Layer Security protocol Version 1.0 (TLS 1.0) emerged and was codified by the IETF
280   as RFC 2246 [22]. While TLS 1.0 is based on SSL 3.0, and the differences between them are not
281   dramatic, they are significant enough that TLS 1.0 and SSL 3.0 do not interoperate.

282   TLS 1.1, specified in RFC 4346 [23], was developed to address weaknesses discovered in TLS
283   1.0, primarily in the areas of initialization vector selection and padding error processing.
284   Initialization vectors were made explicit[4] to prevent a certain class of attacks on the Cipher
285   Block Chaining (CBC) mode of operation used by TLS. The handling of padding errors was

---

[2] https://obamawhitehouse.archives.gov/sites/default/files/omb/memoranda/2015/m-15-13.pdf

[3] See https://https.cio.gov/ for more details on this initiative.

[4] The initialization vector (IV) must be sent; it cannot be derived from a state known by both parties, such as the previous
   message.

286   altered to treat a padding error as a bad message authentication code, rather than a decryption
287   failure. In addition, the TLS 1.1 RFC acknowledges attacks on CBC mode that rely on the time
288   to compute the message authentication code (MAC). The TLS 1.1 specification states that to
289   defend against such attacks, an implementation must process records in the same manner
290   regardless of whether padding errors exist. Further implementation considerations for CBC
291   modes (which were not included in RFC 4346 [23]) are discussed in Section 3.3.2.

292   TLS 1.2, specified in RFC 5246 [24], made several cryptographic enhancements, particularly in
293   the area of hash functions, with the ability to use or specify the SHA-2 family algorithms for
294   hash, MAC, and Pseudorandom Function (PRF) computations. TLS 1.2 also adds authenticated
295   encryption with associated data (AEAD) cipher suites.

296   TLS 1.3, specified in RFC 8446 [50], represents a significant change to TLS that aims to address
297   threats that have arisen over the years. Among the changes are a new handshake protocol, a new
298   key derivation process that uses the HMAC-based Extract-and-Expand Key Derivation Function
299   (HKDF) [36], and the removal of cipher suites that use static RSA or DH key exchanges, the
300   CBC mode of operation, or SHA-1. Many extensions defined for use with TLS 1.2 and below
301   cannot be used with TLS 1.3.

302   1.2   Scope

303   Security is not a single property possessed by a single protocol. Rather, security includes a
304   complex set of related properties that together provide the required information assurance
305   characteristics and information protection services. Security requirements are usually derived
306   from a risk assessment of the threats or attacks that an adversary is likely to mount against a
307   system. The adversary is likely to take advantage of implementation vulnerabilities found in
308   many system components, including computer operating systems, application software systems,
309   and the computer networks that interconnect them. Thus, in order to secure a system against a
310   myriad of threats, security must be judiciously placed in the various systems and network layers.

311   These guidelines focus only on network security, and they focus directly on the small portion of
312   the network communications stack that is referred to as the transport layer. Several other NIST
313   publications address security requirements in the other parts of the system and network layers.
314   Adherence to these guidelines only protects the data in transit. Other applicable NIST standards
315   and guidelines should be used to ensure protection of systems and stored data.

316   These guidelines focus on the common use cases where clients and servers must interoperate
317   with a wide variety of implementations, and authentication is performed using public-key
318   certificates. To promote interoperability, implementations often support a wide array of
319   cryptographic options. However, there are much more constrained TLS implementations where
320   security is needed but broad interoperability is not required, and the cost of implementing unused
321   features may be prohibitive. For example, minimal servers are often implemented in embedded
322   controllers and network infrastructure devices such as routers, and then used with browsers to
323   remotely configure and manage the devices. There are also cases where both the client and server
324   for an application's TLS connection are under the control of the same entity, and therefore
325   allowing a variety of options for interoperability is not necessary. The use of an appropriate
326   subset of the capabilities specified in these guidelines may be acceptable in such cases.

327   The scope is further limited to TLS when used in conjunction with TCP/IP. For example,
328   Datagram TLS (DTLS), which operates over datagram protocols, is outside the scope of these
329   guidelines. NIST may issue separate guidelines for DTLS at a later date.

330   **1.2.1   Alternative Configurations**

331   TLS may be used to secure the communications of a wide variety of applications in a diverse set
332   of operating environments. As such, there is not a single configuration that will work well for all
333   scenarios. These guidelines attempt to provide general-use recommendations. However, the
334   needs of an agency or application may differ from general needs. **Deviations from these
335   guidelines are acceptable, provided that agencies and system administrators assess and
336   accept the risks associated with alternative configurations in terms of both security and
337   interoperability.**

338   **1.3   Document Conventions**

339   Throughout this document, key words are used to identify requirements. The key words "**shall**,"
340   "**shall not**," "**should**," and "**should not**" are used. These words are a subset of the IETF Request
341   for Comments (RFC) 2119 key words, and have been chosen based on convention in other
342   normative documents [14]. In addition to the key words, the words "need," "can," and "may" are
343   used in this document, but are not intended to be normative. The key words "NIST-approved"
344   and "NIST-recommended" are used to indicate that a scheme or algorithm is described in a
345   Federal Information Processing Standard (FIPS) or is recommended by NIST.

346   The recommendations in this document are grouped by server recommendations and client
347   recommendations. Section 3 provides detailed guidance for the selection and configuration of
348   TLS servers. Section 4 provides detailed guidance for the selection, configuration, and use of
349   TLS clients.

350 **2   TLS Overview**

351 TLS exchanges records via the TLS record protocol. A TLS record contains several fields,
352 including version information, application protocol data, and the higher-level protocol used to
353 process the application data. TLS protects the application data by using a set of cryptographic
354 algorithms to ensure the confidentiality, integrity, and authenticity of exchanged application data.
355 TLS defines several protocols for connection management that sit on top of the record protocol,
356 where each protocol has its own record type. These protocols, discussed in Section 2.1, are used
357 to establish and change security parameters, and to communicate error and warning conditions to
358 the server and client. Sections 2.2 through 2.6 describe the security services provided by the TLS
359 protocol and how those security services are provisioned. Section 2.7 discusses key management.

360 **2.1   TLS Subprotocols**

361 There are three subprotocols in the TLS protocol that are used to control the session connection:
362 the handshake, change cipher spec, and alert protocols. The TLS handshake protocol is used to
363 negotiate the session parameters. The alert protocol is used to notify the other party of an error
364 condition. The change cipher spec protocol is used in TLS 1.0, 1.1, and 1.2 to change the
365 cryptographic parameters of a session. In addition, the client and the server exchange application
366 data that is protected by the security services provisioned by the negotiated cipher suite. These
367 security services are negotiated and established with the handshake.

368 The handshake protocol consists of a series of message exchanges between the client and the
369 server. The handshake protocol initializes both the client and server to use cryptographic
370 capabilities by negotiating a cipher suite of algorithms and functions, including key
371 establishment, digital signature, confidentiality and integrity algorithms. Clients and servers can
372 be configured so that one or more of the following security services are negotiated during the
373 handshake: confidentiality, message integrity, authentication, and replay protection. A
374 confidentiality service provides assurance that data is kept secret, preventing eavesdropping. A
375 message integrity service provides confirmation that unauthorized data modification is detected,
376 thus preventing undetected deletion, addition, or modification of data. An authentication service
377 provides assurance of the sender or receiver's identity, thereby detecting forgery. Replay
378 protection ensures that an unauthorized user does not capture and successfully replay previous
379 data. In order to comply with these guidelines, both the client and the server must be configured
380 for data confidentiality and integrity services.

381 The handshake protocol is used to optionally exchange X.509 public-key certificates[5] to
382 authenticate the server and the client to each other.

383 The handshake protocol is responsible for establishing the session parameters. The client and
384 server negotiate algorithms for authentication, confidentiality and integrity, as well as derive
385 symmetric keys and establish other session parameters, such as extensions. The negotiated set of
386 cryptographic algorithms is called the cipher suite.

_____

[5] In these guidelines, the terms "certificate" and "public-key certificate" are used interchangeably.

387   Alerts are used to convey information about the session, such as errors or warnings. For example,
388   an alert can be used to signal a decryption error (decrypt_error) or that access has been denied
389   (access_denied). Some alerts are used for warnings, and others are considered fatal and lead to
390   immediate termination of the session. A close_notify alert message is used to signal normal
391   termination of a session. Like all other messages after the handshake protocol is completed, alert
392   messages are encrypted (and optionally compressed in TLS versions prior to TLS 1.3).

393   Details of the handshake, change cipher spec (in TLS versions prior to 1.3), and alert protocols
394   are outside the scope of these guidelines; they are described in RFC 5246 [24] and RFC 8446
395   [50].

396   2.2   Shared Secret Negotiation

397   The client and server establish keying material during the TLS handshake protocol. The
398   derivation of the premaster secret depends on the key exchange method that is agreed upon and
399   the version of TLS used. For example, when Diffie-Hellman is used as the key-exchange
400   algorithm in TLS 1.2 and earlier versions, the client and server send each other their parameters,
401   which are used to compute the premaster secret. The premaster secret, along with random values
402   exchanged by the client and server in the hello messages, is used in a pseudorandom function
403   (PRF) to compute the master secret. In TLS 1.3, the master secret is derived by iteratively
404   invoking an extract-then-expand function with previously derived secrets. The master secret is
405   used to derive session keys, which are used by the negotiated security services to protect the data
406   exchanged between the client and the server, thus providing a secure channel for the client and
407   the server to communicate.

408   The establishment of these secrets is secure against eavesdroppers. When the TLS protocol is
409   used in accordance with these guidelines, the application data, as well as the secrets, are not
410   vulnerable to attackers who place themselves in the middle of the connection. The attacker
411   cannot modify the handshake messages without being detected by the client and the server
412   because the Finished message, which is exchanged after security parameter establishment,
413   provides integrity protection to the entire exchange. In other words, an attacker cannot modify or
414   downgrade the security of the connection by placing itself in the middle of the negotiation.

415   2.3   Confidentiality

416   Confidentiality is provided for a communication session by the negotiated encryption algorithm
417   for the cipher suite and the encryption keys derived from the master secret and random values,
418   one for encryption by the client (the client write key), and another for encryption by the server
419   (the server write key). The sender of a message (client or server) encrypts the message using a
420   derived encryption key; the receiver uses the same (independently derived) key to decrypt the
421   message. Both the client and server know these keys, and decrypt the messages using the same
422   key that was used for encryption. The encryption keys are derived from the shared master secret.

423   2.4   Integrity

424   The keyed MAC algorithm, specified by the negotiated cipher suite, provides message integrity.
425   As with confidentiality, there is a different key for each direction of communication. The sender
426   of a message (client or server) calculates the MAC for the message using the appropriate MAC

427 key. When the receiver processes the message, it calculates its own version of the MAC using
428 the MAC algorithm and sender's MAC key. The receiver verifies that the MAC that it calculates
429 matches the MAC sent by the sender.

430 Two types of constructions are used for MAC algorithms in TLS. TLS versions 1.0, 1.1 and 1.2
431 support the use of the Keyed-Hash Message Authentication Code (HMAC) using the hash
432 algorithm specified by the negotiated cipher suite. With HMAC, MACs for server-to-client
433 messages are keyed by the server write MAC key, while MACs for client-to-server messages
434 are keyed by the client write MAC key. These MAC keys are derived from the shared master
435 secret.

436 TLS 1.2 added AEAD cipher modes of operation, such as Counter with CBC-MAC (CCM) [40]
437 and Galois Counter Mode (GCM) [49, 53], as an alternative way of providing integrity and
438 confidentiality. In AEAD modes, the sender uses its write key for both encryption and integrity
439 protection. The client and server write MAC keys are not used. The recipient decrypts the
440 message and verifies the integrity information using the sender's write key. In TLS 1.3, only
441 AEAD symmetric algorithms are used for confidentiality and integrity.

442 **2.5 Authentication**

443 Server authentication is performed by the client using the server's public-key certificate, which
444 the server presents during the handshake. The exact nature of the cryptographic operation for
445 server authentication is dependent on the negotiated security parameters and extensions. In many
446 cases, authentication is performed explicitly by verifying digital signatures using public keys that
447 are present in certificates, and implicitly by the use of the server public key by the client during
448 the establishment of the master secret. A successful Finished message implies that both parties
449 calculated the same master secret and thus, the server must have known the private key
450 corresponding to the public key in the server's certificate.

451 Client authentication is optional, and only occurs at the server's request. Client authentication is
452 based on the client's public-key certificate. The exact nature of the cryptographic operation for
453 client authentication depends on the negotiated cipher suite's key-exchange algorithm and the
454 negotiated extensions. For example, when the client's public-key certificate contains an RSA
455 public key, the client signs a portion of the handshake message using the private key
456 corresponding to that public key, and the server verifies the signature using the public key to
457 authenticate the client.

458 **2.6 Anti-Replay**

459 TLS provides inherent protection against replay attacks, except when 0-RTT data (optionally
460 sent in the first flight of handshake messages) is sent in TLS 1.3.[6] The integrity-protected
461 envelope of the message contains a monotonically increasing sequence number. Once the
462 message integrity is verified, the sequence number of the current message is compared with the

---

[6] While TLS 1.3 does not inherently provide replay protection with 0-RTT data, the TLS 1.3 specification does recommend mechanisms to protect against replay attacks (see Section 8 of [50]).

463 sequence number of the previous message. The sequence number of the current message must be
464 greater than the sequence number of the previous message in order to further process the
465 message.

466 **2.7 Key Management**

467 The security of the server's private key is critical to the security of TLS. If the server's private
468 key is weak or can be obtained by a third party, the third party can masquerade as the server to
469 all clients. Similarly, if a third party can obtain a public-key certificate for a public key
470 corresponding to its own private key in the name of a legitimate server from a certification
471 authority (CA) trusted by the clients, the third party can masquerade as the server to the clients.
472 Requirements and recommendations to mitigate these concerns are addressed later in these
473 guidelines.

474 Similar threats exist for clients. If a client's private key is weak or can be obtained by a third
475 party, the third party can masquerade as the client to a server. Similarly, if a third party can
476 obtain a public-key certificate for a public key corresponding to his own private key in the name
477 of a client from a CA trusted by the server, the third party can masquerade as that client to the
478 server. Requirements and recommendations to mitigate these concerns are addressed later in
479 these guidelines.

480 Since the random numbers generated by the client and server contribute to the randomness of the
481 session keys, the client and server must be capable of generating random numbers with at least
482 112 bits of security[7] each. The various TLS session keys derived from these random values and
483 other data are valid for the duration of the session. Because the session keys are only used to
484 protect messages exchanged during an active TLS session, and are not used to protect any data at
485 rest, there is no requirement for recovering TLS session keys. However, all versions of TLS
486 provide mechanisms to store a key related to a session, which allow sessions to be resumed in the
487 future. Keys for a resumed session are derived during an abbreviated handshake that uses the
488 stored key as a form of authentication.

489

---

[7] See the SP 800-90 series for more information on random bit generators (https://csrc.nist.gov/projects/random-bit-generation)

490 ## 3   Minimum Requirements for TLS Servers

491 This section provides a minimum set of requirements that a server must implement in order to
492 meet these guidelines. Requirements are organized in the following sections: TLS protocol
493 version support; server keys and certificates; cryptographic support; TLS extension support;
494 client authentication; session resumption; compression methods; and operational considerations.

495 Specific requirements are stated as either implementation requirements or configuration
496 requirements. Implementation requirements indicate that Federal agencies **shall not** procure TLS
497 server implementations unless they include the required functionality, or can be augmented with
498 additional commercial products to meet requirements. Configuration requirements indicate that
499 TLS server administrators are required to verify that particular features are enabled or disabled,
500 or in some cases, configured appropriately, if present.

501 ### 3.1   Protocol Version Support

502 Servers that support government-only applications[8] **shall** be configured to use TLS 1.2, and
503 **should** be configured to use TLS 1.3. These servers **should not** be configured to use TLS 1.1,
504 and **shall not** use TLS 1.0, SSL 3.0, or SSL 2.0. TLS versions 1.2 and 1.3 are represented by
505 major and minor number tuples (3, 3) and (3, 4), respectively, and may appear in that format
506 during configuration.[9]

507 Servers that support citizen or business-facing applications (i.e., the client may not be part of a
508 government IT system)[10] **shall** be configured to negotiate TLS 1.2, **should** be configured to
509 negotiate TLS 1.3. The use of TLS versions 1.1 and 1.0 is generally discouraged, but these
510 versions may be configured when necessary to enable interaction with citizens and businesses.
511 See Appendix F for discussion on determining whether to support TLS 1.0 and TLS 1.1. These
512 servers **shall not** allow the use of SSL 2.0 or SSL 3.0.

513 Agencies **shall** support TLS 1.3 by January 1, 2024. After this date, servers **shall** support TLS
514 1.3 for both government-only and citizen or business-facing applications. Note that TLS 1.3 and
515 1.2 are intended to coexist, and should both be enabled after the TLS 1.3 adoption deadline.

516 Some server implementations are known to implement version negotiation incorrectly. For
517 example, there are TLS 1.0 servers that terminate the connection when the client offers a version
518 newer than TLS 1.0. Servers that incorrectly implement TLS version negotiation **shall not** be

---

[8] A government-only application is an application where the intended users are exclusively government employees or contractors working on behalf of the government. This includes applications that are accessed on a government employee's bring-your-own-device (BYOD) system.

[9] Historically TLS 1.0 was assigned major and minor tuple (3,1) to align it as SSL 3.1. TLS 1.1 is represented by the major and minor tuple (3,2).

[10] For the purposes of this document, clients that reside on "bring your own device" (BYOD) systems, or privately-owned systems used to perform telework, are considered to be part of the government IT system, as they access services that are not available to the public.

519   used.

3.2   Server Keys and Certificates

521   The TLS server **shall** be configured with one or more public-key certificates and the associated
522   private keys. TLS server implementations **should** support the use of multiple server certificates
523   with their associated private keys to support algorithm and key size agility.

524   Several options for TLS server certificates meet the requirement for NIST-approved
525   cryptography: an RSA signature certificate; an Elliptic Curve Digital Signature Algorithm
526   (ECDSA) signature certificate; a Digital Signature Algorithm (DSA)[11] signature certificate; a
527   Diffie-Hellman (DH) certificate; and an Elliptic Curve Diffie-Hellman (ECDH) certificate. Note
528   that externally-accessible servers are expected to be configured with ECDSA or RSA certificates
529   (see [67]). The other certificate types, and their associated cipher suites, are included in these
530   guidelines for completeness and to cover edge cases.

531   At a minimum, TLS servers conforming to this specification **shall** be configured with an RSA
532   signature certificate or an ECDSA signature certificate. If the server is configured with an
533   ECDSA signature certificate, either curve P-256 or curve P-384 **should** be used for the public
534   key in the certificate.[12]

535   TLS servers **shall** be configured with certificates issued by a CA. Furthermore, TLS server
536   certificates **shall** be issued by a CA that publishes revocation information in Online Certificate
537   Status Protocol (OCSP) [55] responses. The CA may additionally publish revocation information
538   in a certificate revocation list (CRL) [18]. The source(s) for the revocation information **shall** be
539   included in the CA-issued certificate in the appropriate extension to promote interoperability.

540   A TLS server that has been issued certificates by multiple CAs can select the appropriate
541   certificate based on the client specified "Trusted CA Keys" TLS extension (see Section 3.4.2.7).
542   A TLS server that has been issued certificates for multiple server names can select the
543   appropriate certificate based on the client specified "Server Name" TLS extension (see Section
544   3.4.1.2). A TLS server certificate may also contain multiple names in the Subject Alternative
545   Name extension in order to allow the use of multiple server names of the same name form (e.g.,
546   DNS name) or multiple server names of multiple name forms (e.g., DNS names, IP address,
547   etc.).

548   Application processes for obtaining certificates differ and require different levels of proof when
549   associating certificates to domains. An applicant can obtain a domain-validated (DV) certificate
550   by proving control over a DNS domain. An Organization Validation (OV) certificate requires
551   further vetting. An Extended Validation (EV) certificate has the most thorough identity vetting

---

[11] In the names for the TLS cipher suites, DSA is referred to as DSS (Digital Signature Standard), for historical reasons.

[12] The recommended elliptic curves now listed in FIPS 186-4 [62] will be moved to SP 800-186. Until SP 800-186 is published, the recommended elliptic curves should be taken from FIPS 186-4.

552   process. This recommendation does not provide guidance on which verification level to use.

553   Section 3.2.1 specifies a detailed profile for server certificates. Basic guidelines for RSA,
554   ECDSA, DSA, DH, and ECDH certificates are provided. Section 3.2.2 specifies requirements for
555   revocation checking. Section 3.5.4 specifies requirements for the "hints list."

3.2.1   Server Certificate Profile

557   The server certificate profile, described in this section, provides requirements and
558   recommendations for the format of the server certificate. To comply with these guidelines, the
559   TLS server certificate **shall** be an X.509 version 3 certificate; both the public key contained in
560   the certificate and the signature **shall** provide at least 112 bits of security. Prior to TLS 1.2, the
561   server Certificate message required that the signing algorithm for the certificate be the same as
562   the algorithm for the certificate key (see Section 7.4.2 of [23]). If the server supports TLS
563   versions prior to TLS 1.2, the certificate **should** be signed with an algorithm consistent with the
564   public key:[13,14]

- Certificates containing RSA, ECDSA, or DSA public keys **should** be signed with those same signature algorithms, respectively;

- Certificates containing Diffie-Hellman public keys **should** be signed with DSA; and

- Certificates containing ECDH public keys **should** be signed with ECDSA.

569   The extended key usage extension limits how the keys in a certificate are used. There is a key
570   purpose specifically for server authentication, and the server **should** be configured to allow its
571   use. The use of the extended key usage extension will facilitate successful server authentication,
572   as some clients may require the presence of an extended key usage extension. The use of the
573   server DNS name in the Subject Alternative Name field ensures that any name constraints on the
574   certification path will be properly enforced.

575   The server certificate profile is listed in Table 3-1. In the absence of agency-specific certificate
576   profile requirements, this certificate profile **should** be used for the server certificate.

577   **Table 3-1: TLS Server Certificate Profile**

Field	Critical	Value	Description
Version	N/A	2	Version 3
Serial Number	N/A	Unique positive integer	Must be unique

---

[13] This recommendation is an artifact of requirements in TLS 1.0 and 1.1.

[14] Algorithm-dependent guidelines exist for the generation of public and private key pairs. For guidance on the generation of DH and ECDH key pairs, see SP 800-56A [7]. For guidance regarding the generation of RSA, DSA and ECDSA key pairs, see [62].

Field	Critical	Value	Description
Issuer Signature Algorithm	N/A	*Values by CA key type:*	
		sha256WithRSAEncryption {1 2 840 113549 1 1 11}, or stronger	CA with RSA key
		id-RSASSA-PSS {1 2 840 113549 1 1 10 }	CA with RSA key
		ecdsa-with-SHA256 {1 2 840 10045 4 3 2}, or stronger	CA with elliptic curve key
		id-dsa-with-sha256 {2 16 840 1 101 3 4 3 2}, or stronger	CA with DSA key
Issuer Distinguished Name (DN)	N/A	Unique X.500 issuing CA DN	A single value **shall** be encoded in each Relative Distinguished Name (RDN). All attributes that are of DirectoryString type **shall** be encoded as a PrintableString.
Validity Period	N/A	3 years or less	Dates through 2049 expressed in UTCTime
Subject Distinguished Name	N/A	Unique X.500 subject DN per agency requirements	A single value **shall** be encoded in each RDN. All attributes that are of DirectoryString type **shall** be encoded as a PrintableString. If present, the CN attribute **shall** be of the form: CN={host IP address | host DNS name}
Field	**Critical**	**Value**	**Description**
Subject Public Key Information	N/A	*Values by certificate type:*	
		rsaEncryption {1 2 840 113549 1 1 1}	RSA signature certificate 2048-bit RSA key modulus, or other approved lengths as defined in [62] and [5] Parameters: NULL
		ecPublicKey {1 2 840 10045 2 1}	ECDSA signature certificate or ECDH certificate Parameters: namedCurve OID for named curve specified in SP 800-186.[15] The curve **should** be P-256 or P-384 SubjectPublic Key: Uncompressed EC Point.
		id-dsa {1 2 840 10040 4 1}	DSA signature certificate Parameters: p, q, g (2048-bit large prime, i.e., p)
		dhpublicnumber {1 2 840 10046 2 1}	DH certificate Parameters: p, g, q (2048-bit large prime, i.e., p)
Issuer's Signature	N/A	Same value as in Issuer Signature Algorithm	
Extensions			

---

[15] The recommended elliptic curves now listed in FIPS 186-4 [62] will be moved to SP 800-186. Until SP 800-186 is published, the recommended elliptic curves should be taken from FIPS 186-4.

Field	Critical	Value	Description
Authority Key Identifier	No	Octet String	Same as subject key identifier in issuing CA certificate Prohibited: Issuer DN, Serial Number tuple
Subject Key Identifier	No	Octet String	Same as in PKCS-10 request or calculated by the issuing CA
Key Usage	Yes	*Values by certificate type:*	
		digitalSignature	RSA signature certificate, ECDSA signature certificate, or DSA signature certificate
		keyAgreement	ECDH certificate, DH certificate
Extended Key Usage	No	id-kp-serverAuth {1 3 6 1 5 5 7 3 1}	Required
		id-kp-clientAuth {1 3 6 1 5 5 7 3 2}	Optional
			Prohibited: anyExtendedKeyUsage; all others unless consistent with key usage extension
Certificate Policies	No		Optional
Subject Alternative Name	No	DNS host name, or IP address if there is no DNS name assigned	Required. Multiple SANs are permitted, e.g., for load balanced environments.
Authority Information Access	No	id-ad-caIssuers	Required. Access method entry contains HTTP URL for certificates issued to issuing CA
		id-ad-ocsp	Required. Access method entry contains HTTP URL for the issuing CA OCSP responder
CRL Distribution Points	No	See comments	Optional. HTTP value in distributionPoint field pointing to a full and complete CRL. Prohibited: reasons and cRLIssuer fields, and nameRelativetoCRLIssuer CHOICE
Signed Certificate Timestamps List	No	See comments	Optional. This extension contains a sequence of Signed Certificate Timestamps, which provide evidence that the certificate has been submitted to Certificate Transparency logs.
TLS feature	No	status_request(5)	Optional. This extension (sometimes referred to as the "must staple" extension) may be present to indicate to clients that the server supports OCSP stapling and will provide a stapled OCSP response when one is requested.

578

3.2.2　Obtaining Revocation Status Information for the Client Certificate

580 The server **shall** perform revocation checking of the client certificate when client authentication
581 is used. Revocation information **shall** be obtained by the server from one or more of the
582 following locations:

583　　1. Certificate Revocation List (CRL) or OCSP [55] response in the server's local store;

584　　2. OCSP response from a locally configured OCSP responder;

585   3. OCSP response from the OCSP responder location identified in the OCSP field in the
586   Authority Information Access extension in the client certificate; or

587   4. CRL from the CRL Distribution Points extension in the client certificate.

588   When the local store does not have the current or a cogent[16] CRL or OCSP response, and the
589   OCSP responder and the CRL distribution point are unavailable or inaccessible at the time of
590   TLS session establishment, the server will either deny the connection or accept a potentially
591   revoked or compromised certificate. The decision to accept or reject a certificate in this situation
592   **should** be made according to agency policy.

593   ### 3.2.3 Server Public-Key Certificate Assurance

594   The policies, procedures, and security controls under which a public-key certificate is issued by a
595   CA are documented in a certificate policy. The use of a certificate policy that is designed with
596   the secure operation of PKI in mind and adherence to the stipulated certificate policy mitigates
597   the threat that the issuing CA can be compromised or that the registration system, persons or
598   process can be compromised to obtain an unauthorized certificate in the name of a legitimate
599   entity, and thus compromise the clients. With this in mind, the CA Browser Forum, a private-
600   sector organization, has carried out some efforts in this area by writing requirements for issuing
601   certificates from publicly trusted CAs in order for those CAs and their trust anchor to remain in
602   browser trust stores [15]. Under another effort, the CA Browser Forum has written guidelines for
603   issuing Extended Validation Certificates [16].

604   Several concepts are under development that further mitigate the risks associated with the
605   compromise of a CA or X.509 certificate registration system, process or personnel. These
606   include the Certificate Transparency project (see Section 3.4.2.11) and other emerging concepts,
607   which are discussed in Appendix E.

608   The policy under which a certificate has been issued may optionally be represented in the
609   certificate using the certificatePolicies extension, specified in [18] and updated in [70]. When
610   used, one or more certificate policy object identifiers (OID) are asserted in this extension, with
611   each OID representing a specific certificate policy. Many TLS clients (e.g., browsers), however,
612   do not offer the ability to accept or reject certificates based on the policies under which they
613   were issued. Therefore, it is generally necessary for TLS server certificates to be issued by CAs
614   that only issue certificates in accordance with a certificate policy that specifies adequate security
615   controls.

616   When an agency is obtaining a certificate for a TLS server for which all the clients are under the
617   agency's control, the agency may issue the certificate from its own CA if it can configure the
618   clients to trust that CA. In other cases, the agency should obtain a certificate from a publicly-
619   trusted CA (a CA that clients that will be connecting to the server have already been configured

---

[16] A CRL is considered "cogent" when the "CRL Scope" [18] is appropriate for the certificate in question.

620   to trust).

3.3   Cryptographic Support

622   Cryptographic support in TLS is provided through the use of various cipher suites. A cipher suite
623   specifies a collection of algorithms for key exchange (in TLS 1.2 and earlier only),[17] and for
624   providing confidentiality and integrity services to application data. The cipher suite negotiation
625   occurs during the TLS handshake protocol. The client presents cipher suites that it supports to
626   the server, and the server selects one of them to secure the session data.

627   In addition to the selection of appropriate cipher suites, system administrators may also have
628   additional considerations specific to the implementation of the cryptographic algorithms, as well
629   as cryptographic module validation requirements. Acceptable cipher suites are listed in Section
630   3.3.1, grouped by certificate type and protocol version. Implementation considerations are
631   discussed in Section 3.3.2, and recommendations regarding cryptographic module validation are
632   described in Section 3.3.3.

3.3.1   Cipher Suites

634   Cipher suites specify the cryptographic algorithms that will be used for a session. Cipher suites
635   in TLS 1.0 through TLS 1.2 have the form:

636   TLS_*KeyExchangeAlg*_WITH_*EncryptionAlg_MessageAuthenticationAlg*

637   For example, the cipher suite TLS_ECDHE_RSA_WITH_AES_128_CBC_SHA uses ephemeral
638   ECDH key establishment, with parameters signed using RSA, confidentiality is provided by
639   AES-128 in cipher block chaining mode, and message authentication is performed using
640   HMAC_SHA.[18] For further information on cipher suite interpretation, see Appendix B.

641   Cipher suites are defined differently in TLS 1.3. These cipher suites do not specify the key
642   exchange algorithm, and have the form:

643   TLS_*AEAD_HASH*

644   For example, the cipher suite TLS_AES_128_GCM_SHA256 uses AES-128 in Galois Counter
645   Mode for confidentiality and message authentication, and uses SHA-256 for the PRF. TLS 1.3
646   cipher suites cannot be used for TLS 1.2 connections, and TLS 1.2 cipher suites cannot be
647   negotiated with TLS 1.3.

648   When negotiating a cipher suite, the client sends a handshake message with a list of cipher suites
649   it will accept. The server chooses from the list and sends a handshake message back indicating
650   which cipher suite it will accept. Although the client may order the list with what it considers to
651   be the strongest cipher suites listed first, the server may ignore the preference order and choose

---

[17] In TLS 1.3 the key exchange algorithm is specified solely in extensions (see Sections 3.4.2.3 and 3.4.2.10).

[18] SHA indicates the use of the SHA-1 hash algorithm.

652　*any* of the cipher suites proposed by the client. The server may have its own cipher suite
653　preference order, and it may be different from the client's. Therefore, there is *no* guarantee that
654　the negotiation will settle on the strongest common suite. If no cipher suites are common to the
655　client and server, the connection is aborted.

656　The server **shall** be configured to only use cipher suites that are composed entirely of NIST-
657　approved algorithms (i.e., [6, 7, 9, 25-27, 61-63, 65]). A complete list of acceptable cipher suites
658　for general use is provided in this section, grouped by certificate type and TLS protocol version.
659　The Internet Assigned Numbers Authority (IANA) value for each cipher suite is given after its
660　text description, in parentheses.[19]

661　In some situations, such as closed environments, it may be appropriate to use pre-shared keys.
662　Pre-shared keys are symmetric keys that are already in place prior to the initiation of a TLS
663　session, which are used in the derivation of the premaster secret. For cipher suites that are
664　acceptable in pre-shared key environments, see Appendix C.

665　NIST is deprecating the use of RSA key transport as used in TLS. Some applications or
666　environments may require the use of RSA key transport during a transition period. Acceptable
667　cipher suites for use in this situation are located in Appendix D.

668　The following cipher suite listings are grouped by certificate type and TLS protocol version. The
669　cipher suites in these lists include the cipher suites that contain NIST-approved cryptographic
670　algorithms. Cipher suites that do not appear in this section, Appendix C, or Appendix D **shall**
671　**not** be used.

672　Cipher suites using ephemeral DH and ephemeral ECDH (i.e., those with DHE or ECDHE in the
673　second mnemonic) provide perfect forward secrecy.[20] When ephemeral keys are used to establish
674　the master secret, each ephemeral key-pair (i.e., the server ephemeral key-pair and the client
675　ephemeral key-pair) **shall** have at least 112 bits of security.

676　3.3.1.1　Cipher Suites for TLS 1.2 and Earlier Versions

677　The first revision of this guidance required support for a small set of cipher suites to promote
678　interoperability and align with TLS specifications. There are no longer any mandatory cipher
679　suite requirements. Cipher suites that comprise AES and other NIST-approved algorithms are
680　acceptable to use, although they are not necessarily equal in terms of security. Cipher suites that
681　use TDEA (3DES) are no longer allowed, due to the limited amounts of data that can be
682　processed under a single key. The server **shall** be configured to only use cipher suites for which
683　it has a valid certificate containing a signature providing at least 112 bits of security.

684　By removing requirements that specific cipher suites be supported, system administrators have

---

[19] The full list of IANA values for TLS parameters can be found at https://www.iana.org/assignments/tls-parameters/tls-parameters.xhtml.

[20] Perfect forward secrecy is the condition in which the compromise of a long-term private key used in deriving a session key subsequent to the derivation does not cause the compromise of the session key.

685　more freedom to meet the needs of their environment and applications. It also increases agility
686　by allowing administrators to immediately disable cipher suites when attacks are discovered
687　without breaking compliance.

688　If a subset of the cipher suites that are acceptable for the server certificate(s) are supported, the
689　following list gives general guidance on choosing the strongest options:

690　　1.　Prefer ephemeral keys over static keys (i.e., prefer DHE over DH, and prefer ECDHE
691　　　　over ECDH). Ephemeral keys provide perfect forward secrecy.
692　　2.　Prefer GCM or CCM modes over CBC mode. The use of an authenticated encryption
693　　　　mode prevents several attacks (see Section 3.3.2 for more information). Note that these
694　　　　are not available in versions prior to TLS 1.2.
695　　3.　Prefer CCM over CCM_8. The latter contains a shorter authentication tag, which
696　　　　provides a lower authentication strength.

697　This list does not have to be strictly followed, as some environments or applications may
698　have special circumstances. Note that this list may become outdated if an attack emerges on
699　one of the preferred components. If an attack significantly impacts the recommended cipher
700　suites, NIST will address the issue in an announcement on the NIST Computer Security
701　Resource Center website (https://csrc.nist.gov).

702　### 3.3.1.1.1　Cipher Suites for ECDSA Certificates

703　TLS version 1.2 includes authenticated encryption modes, and support for the SHA-256 and
704　SHA-384 hash algorithms, which are not supported in prior versions of TLS. These cipher suites
705　are described in [53] and [49]. TLS 1.2 servers that are configured with ECDSA certificates may
706　be configured to support the following cipher suites, which are only supported by TLS 1.2:

707　　•　TLS_ECDHE_ECDSA_WITH_AES_128_GCM_SHA256 (0xC0, 0x2B)
708　　•　TLS_ECDHE_ECDSA_WITH_AES_256_GCM_SHA384 (0xC0, 0x2C)
709　　•　TLS_ECDHE_ECDSA_WITH_AES_128_CCM (0xC0, 0xAC)
710　　•　TLS_ECDHE_ECDSA_WITH_AES_256_CCM (0xC0, 0xAD)
711　　•　TLS_ECDHE_ECDSA_WITH_AES_128_CCM_8 (0xC0, 0xAE)
712　　•　TLS_ECDHE_ECDSA_WITH_AES_256_CCM_8 (0xC0, 0xAF)
713　　•　TLS_ECDHE_ECDSA_WITH_AES_128_CBC_SHA256 (0xC0, 0x23)
714　　•　TLS_ECDHE_ECDSA_WITH_AES_256_CBC_SHA384 (0xC0, 0x24)

715　TLS servers may be configured to support the following cipher suites when ECDSA certificates
716　are used with TLS versions 1.2, 1.1, or 1.0:

717　　•　TLS_ECDHE_ECDSA_WITH_AES_128_CBC_SHA[21] (0xC0, 0x09)

---

[21] In TLS versions 1.0 and 1.1, DHE and ECDHE cipher suites use SHA-1 for signature generation on the ephemeral parameters
(including keys) in the ServerKeyExchange message. While the use of SHA-1 for digital signature generation is generally
disallowed by [10], exceptions can be granted by protocol-specific guidance. SHA-1 is allowed for generating digital
signatures on ephemeral parameters in TLS. Due to the random nature of the ephemeral keys, a third party is unlikely to
cause effective collision. The server and client do not have anything to gain by causing a collision for the connection.
Because of the client random and server random values, the server, the client, or a third party cannot use a colliding set of

718   •   TLS_ECDHE_ECDSA_WITH_AES_256_CBC_SHA (0xC0, 0x0A)

719   **3.3.1.1.2 Cipher Suites for RSA Certificates**

720   TLS 1.2 servers that are configured with RSA certificates may be configured to support the
721   following cipher suites:

722   •   TLS_ECDHE_RSA_WITH_AES_128_GCM_SHA256 (0xC0, 0x2F)
723   •   TLS_ECDHE_RSA_WITH_AES_256_GCM_SHA384 (0xC0, 0x30)
724   •   TLS_DHE_RSA_WITH_AES_128_GCM_SHA256 (0x00, 0x9E)
725   •   TLS_DHE_RSA_WITH_AES_256_GCM_SHA384 (0x00, 0x9F)
726   •   TLS_DHE_RSA_WITH_AES_128_CCM (0xC0, 0x9E)
727   •   TLS_DHE_RSA_WITH_AES_256_CCM (0xC0, 0x9F)
728   •   TLS_DHE_RSA_WITH_AES_128_CCM_8 (0xC0, 0xA2)
729   •   TLS_DHE_RSA_WITH_AES_256_CCM_8 (0xC0, 0xA3)
730   •   TLS_ECDHE_RSA_WITH_AES_128_CBC_SHA256 (0xC0, 0x27)
731   •   TLS_ECDHE_RSA_WITH_AES_256_CBC_SHA384 (0xC0, 0x28)
732   •   TLS_DHE_RSA_WITH_AES_128_CBC_SHA256 (0x00, 0x67)
733   •   TLS_DHE_RSA_WITH_AES_256_CBC_SHA256 (0x00, 0x6B)

734   TLS servers may be configured to support the following cipher suites when RSA certificates are
735   used with TLS versions 1.2, 1.1, or 1.0:

736   •   TLS_ECDHE_RSA_WITH_AES_128_CBC_SHA (0xC0, 0x13)
737   •   TLS_ECDHE_RSA_WITH_AES_256_CBC_SHA (0xC0, 0x14)
738   •   TLS_DHE_RSA_WITH_AES_128_CBC_SHA (0x00, 0x33)
739   •   TLS_DHE_RSA_WITH_AES_256_CBC_SHA (0x00, 0x39)

740   **3.3.1.1.3 Cipher Suites for DSA Certificates**

741   TLS 1.2 servers that are configured with DSA certificates may be configured to support the
742   following cipher suites:

743   •   TLS_DHE_DSS_WITH_AES_128_GCM_SHA256 (0x00, 0xA2)
744   •   TLS_DHE_DSS_WITH_AES_256_GCM_SHA384 (0x00, 0xA3)
745   •   TLS_DHE_DSS_WITH_AES_128_CBC_SHA256 (0x00, 0x40)
746   •   TLS_DHE_DSS_WITH_AES_256_CBC_SHA256 (0x00, 0x6A)

747   TLS servers may be configured to support the following cipher suites when DSA certificates are
748   used with TLS versions 1.2, 1.1, or 1.0:

749   •   TLS_DHE_DSS_WITH_AES_128_CBC_SHA (0x00, 0x32)

---

messages to masquerade as the client or server in future connections. Any modification to the parameters by a third party during the handshake will ultimately result in a failed connection.

750   • TLS_DHE_DSS_WITH_AES_256_CBC_SHA (0x00, 0x38)

751   **3.3.1.1.4 Cipher Suites for DH Certificates**

752   DH certificates contain a static key, and are signed using either DSA or RSA. Unlike cipher
753   suites that use ephemeral DH, these cipher suites contain static DH parameters. While the use of
754   static keys is technically acceptable, the use of ephemeral key cipher suites is encouraged and
755   preferred over the use of the cipher suites listed in this section.

756   TLS 1.2 servers that are configured with DSA-signed DH certificates may be configured to
757   support the following cipher suites:

758   • TLS_DH_DSS_WITH_AES_128_GCM_SHA256 (0x00, 0xA4)
759   • TLS_DH_DSS_WITH_AES_256_GCM_SHA384 (0x00, 0xA5)
760   • TLS_DH_DSS_WITH_AES_128_CBC_SHA256 (0x00, 0x3E)
761   • TLS_DH_DSS_WITH_AES_256_CBC_SHA256 (0x00, 0x68)

762   TLS servers may be configured to support the following cipher suites when DSA-signed DH
763   certificates are used with TLS versions 1.2, 1.1, or 1.0:

764   • TLS_DH_DSS_WITH_AES_128_CBC_SHA (0x00, 0x30)
765   • TLS_DH_DSS_WITH_AES_256_CBC_SHA (0x00, 0x36)

766   TLS 1.2 servers that are configured with RSA-signed DH certificates may be configured to
767   support the following cipher suites:

768   • TLS_DH_RSA_WITH_AES_128_GCM_SHA256 (0x00, 0xA0)
769   • TLS_DH_RSA_WITH_AES_256_GCM_SHA384 (0x00, 0xA1)
770   • TLS_DH_RSA_WITH_AES_128_CBC_SHA256 (0x00, 0x3F)
771   • TLS_DH_RSA_WITH_AES_256_CBC_SHA256 (0x00, 0x69)

772   TLS servers may be configured to support the following cipher suites when RSA-signed DH
773   certificates are used with TLS versions 1.2, 1.1, or 1.0:

774   • TLS_DH_RSA_WITH_AES_128_CBC_SHA (0x00, 0x31)
775   • TLS_DH_RSA_WITH_AES_256_CBC_SHA (0x00, 0x37)

776   **3.3.1.1.5 Cipher Suites for ECDH Certificates**

777   ECDH certificates contain a static key, and are signed using either ECDSA or RSA. Unlike
778   cipher suites that use ephemeral ECDH, these cipher suites contain static ECDH parameters. The
779   use of ephemeral key cipher suites is encouraged and preferred over the use of the cipher suites
780   listed in this section.

781   TLS 1.2 servers that are configured with ECDSA-signed ECDH certificates may be configured
782   to support the following cipher suites:

783   • TLS_ECDH_ECDSA_WITH_AES_128_GCM_SHA256 (0xC0, 0x2D)
784   • TLS_ECDH_ECDSA_WITH_AES_256_GCM_SHA384 (0xC0, 0x2E)
785   • TLS_ECDH_ECDSA_WITH_AES_128_CBC_SHA256 (0xC0, 0x25)
786   • TLS_ECDH_ECDSA_WITH_AES_256_CBC_SHA384 (0xC0, 0x26)

787   TLS servers may be configured to support the following cipher suites when ECDSA-signed
788   ECDH certificates are used with TLS versions 1.2, 1.1, or 1.0:

789   • TLS_ECDH_ECDSA_WITH_AES_128_CBC_SHA (0xC0, 0x04)
790   • TLS_ECDH_ECDSA_WITH_AES_256_CBC_SHA (0xC0, 0x05)

791   TLS 1.2 servers that are configured with RSA-signed ECDH certificates may be configured to
792   support the following cipher suites:

793   • TLS_ECDH_RSA_WITH_AES_128_GCM_SHA256 (0xC0, 0x31)
794   • TLS_ECDH_RSA_WITH_AES_256_GCM_SHA384 (0xC0, 0x32)
795   • TLS_ECDH_RSA_WITH_AES_128_CBC_SHA256 (0xC0, 0x29)
796   • TLS_ECDH_RSA_WITH_AES_256_CBC_SHA384 (0xC0, 0x2A)

797   TLS servers may be configured to support the following cipher suites when RSA-signed ECDH
798   certificates are used with TLS versions 1.2, 1.1, or 1.0:

799   • TLS_ECDH_RSA_WITH_AES_128_CBC_SHA (0xC0, 0x0E)
800   • TLS_ECDH_RSA_WITH_AES_256_CBC_SHA (0xC0, 0x0F)

801   **3.3.1.2 Cipher Suites for TLS 1.3**

802   TLS 1.3 servers may be configured to support the following cipher suites:

803   • TLS_AES_128_GCM_SHA256 (0x13, 0x01)
804   • TLS_AES_256_GCM_SHA384 (0x13, 0x02)
805   • TLS_AES_128_CCM_SHA256 (0x13, 0x04)
806   • TLS_AES_128_CCM_8_SHA256 (0x13, 0x05)

807   These cipher suites may be used with either RSA or ECDSA server certificates; DSA and DH
808   certificates cannot be used with TLS 1.3. These cipher suites may also be used with pre-shared
809   keys, as specified in Appendix C.

810   **3.3.2 Implementation Considerations**

811   System administrators need to fully understand the ramifications of selecting cipher suites and
812   configuring applications to support only those cipher suites. The security guarantees of the
813   cryptography are limited to the weakest cipher suite supported by the configuration. When
814   configuring an implementation, there are several factors that affect the selection of supported
815   cipher suites.

816   RFC 4346 [23] describes timing attacks on CBC cipher suites, as well as mitigation techniques.
817   TLS implementations **shall** use the bad_record_mac error to indicate a padding error when

818 communications are secured using a CBC cipher suite. Implementations **shall** compute the MAC
819 regardless of whether padding errors exist.

820 In addition to the CBC attacks addressed in RFC 4346 [23], the Lucky 13 attack [1]
821 demonstrates that a constant-time decryption routine is also needed to prevent timing attacks.
822 TLS implementations **should** support constant-time decryption, or near constant-time
823 decryption.

824 The POODLE attack exploits nondeterministic padding in SSL 3.0 [42]. The vulnerability does
825 not exist in the TLS protocols, but the vulnerability can exist in a TLS implementation when the
826 SSL decoder code is reused to process TLS data [37]. TLS implementations **shall** correctly
827 decode the CBC padding bytes.

828 Note that CBC-based attacks can be prevented by using AEAD cipher suites (e.g., GCM, CCM),
829 which are supported in TLS 1.2.

830 ### 3.3.2.1 Algorithm Support

831 Many TLS servers and clients support cipher suites that are not composed of only NIST-
832 approved algorithms. Therefore, it is important that the server is configured to only use NIST-
833 recommended cipher suites. This is particularly important for server implementations that do not
834 allow the server administrator to specify preference order. In such servers, the only way to
835 ensure that a server uses NIST-approved algorithms is to disable cipher suites that use other
836 algorithms.

837 If the server implementation does allow the server administrator to specify a preference, the
838 system administrator is encouraged to use the preference recommendations listed in Section
839 3.3.1.1.

840 ### 3.3.3 Validated Cryptography

841 The cryptographic module used by the server **shall** be a FIPS 140-validated cryptographic
842 module [66]. All cryptographic algorithms that are included in the configured cipher suites **shall**
843 be within the scope of the validation, as well as the random number generator. Note that the TLS
844 1.1 pseudorandom function (PRF) uses MD5 and SHA-1 in parallel so that if one hash function
845 is broken, security is not compromised. While MD5 is not a NIST-approved algorithm, the TLS
846 1.1 PRF is specified as acceptable in SP 800-135 [20]. TLS 1.3 uses the HMAC-based Extract-
847 and-Expand Key Derivation Function (HKDF), described in RFC 5869 [36], to derive the
848 session keys. Note that in TLS versions prior to 1.2, the use of SHA-1 is considered acceptable
849 for signing ephemeral keys and for signing for client authentication. This is due the difficulty for
850 a third party to cause a collision that is not detected. In TLS 1.2, the default hash function in the
851 PRF is SHA-256. Other than the SHA-1 exception listed for specific instances above, all
852 cryptography used **shall** provide at least 112 bits of security. All server and client certificates
853 **shall** contain public keys that offer at least 112 bits of security. All server and client certificates
854 and certificates in their certification paths **shall** be signed using key pairs that offer at least 112
855 bits of security and SHA-224 or a stronger hashing algorithm. All ephemeral keys used by the
856 client and server **shall** offer at least 112 bits of security. All symmetric algorithms used to protect
857 the TLS data **shall** use keys that offer at least 112 bits of security.

858 The FIPS 140 validation certificate for the cryptographic module used by the server **shall**
859 indicate that the random bit generator (RBG) has been validated in accordance with the SP 800-
860 90 series [8, 43, 60].[22]

861 The server random value, sent in the ServerHello message, contains a 4-byte timestamp[23] value
862 and 28-byte random value in TLS version 1.0, 1.1, and 1.2, and contains a 32-byte random value
863 in TLS 1.3. The validated random number generator **shall** be used to generate the random bytes
864 of the server random value.[24] The validated random number generator **should** be used to
865 generate the 4-byte timestamp of the server random value.

866 3.4 TLS Extension Support

867 Several TLS extensions are described in RFCs. This section contains recommendations for a
868 subset of the TLS extensions that the Federal agencies **shall**, **should**, or **should not** use as they
869 become prevalent in commercially available TLS servers and clients.

870 System administrators must carefully consider the risks of supporting extensions that are not
871 listed as mandatory. Only extensions whose specification have an impact on security are
872 discussed here, but the reader is advised that supporting any extension can have unintended
873 security consequences. In particular, enabling extensions increases the potential for
874 implementation flaws and could leave a system vulnerable. For example, the Heartbleed bug [69]
875 was a flaw in an implementation of the heartbeat extension [56]. Although the extension has no
876 inherent security implications, the implementation flaw exposed server data, including private
877 keys, to attackers.

878 In general, it is advised that servers only be configured to support extensions that are required by
879 the application or enhance security. Extensions that are not needed **should not** be enabled.

880 3.4.1 Mandatory TLS Extensions

881 The server **shall** support the use of the following TLS extensions.

882   5. Renegotiation Indication
883   6. Server Name Indication
884   7. Extended Master Secret
885   8. Signature Algorithms
886   9. Certificate Status Request extension

---

[22] Validation will include compliance with SP 800-90C once it is available.

[23] The timestamp value does not need to be correct in TLS. It can be any 4-byte value, unless otherwise restricted by higher-level or application protocols.

[24] TLS 1.3 implementations include a downgrade protection mechanism embedded in the random value that overwrites the last eight bytes of the server random value with a fixed value. When negotiating TLS 1.2, the last eight bytes of the server random will be set to 44 4F 57 4E 47 52 44 01. When TLS 1.1 or below is negotiated, the last eight bytes of the random value will be set to 44 4F 57 4E 47 52 44 00. This overwrite is separate from the validated random bit generator.

887 **3.4.1.1 Renegotiation Indication**

888 *Applies to TLS versions: 1.0, 1.1, 1.2*

889 In TLS versions 1.0 to 1.2, session renegotiation is vulnerable to an attack in which the attacker
890 forms a TLS connection with the target server, injects content of its choice, and then splices in a
891 new TLS connection from a legitimate client. The server treats the legitimate client's initial TLS
892 handshake as a renegotiation of the attacker's negotiated session and thus believes that the initial
893 data transmitted by the attacker is from the legitimate client. The session renegotiation extension
894 is defined to prevent such a session splicing or session interception. The extension uses the
895 concept of cryptographically binding the initial session negotiation and session renegotiation.

896 Server implementations **shall** perform initial and subsequent renegotiations in accordance with
897 RFC 5746 [51] and RFC 8446 [50].

898 **3.4.1.2 Server Name Indication**

899 *Applies to TLS versions: 1.0, 1.1, 1.2, 1.3*

900 Multiple virtual servers may exist at the same network address. The server name indication
901 extension allows the client to specify which of the servers located at the address it is trying to
902 connect with. This extension is available in all versions of TLS. The server **shall** be able to
903 process and respond to the server name indication extension received in a ClientHello message
904 as described in [28].

905 **3.4.1.3 Extended Master Secret**

906 *Applies to TLS versions: 1.0, 1.1, 1.2*

907 Bhargavan et al. have shown that an active attacker can synchronize two TLS sessions such that
908 they share the same master secret, thus allowing the attacker to perform a man-in-the-middle
909 attack [12]. The Extended Master Secret extension, specified in RFC 7627 [35], prevents such
910 attacks by binding the master secret to a hashed log of the full handshake. The server **shall**
911 support the use of this extension.

912 **3.4.1.4 Signature Algorithms**

913 *Applies to TLS versions: 1.2, 1.3*

914 Servers **shall** support the processing of the signature algorithms extension received in a
915 ClientHello message. The extension, its syntax, and processing rules are described in Sections
916 7.4.1.4.1, 7.4.2, and 7.4.3 of RFC 5246 [24] and Section 4.2.3 of RFC 8446 [50]. Note that the
917 extension described in RFC 8446 updates the extension described in RFC 5246 by adding an
918 additional signature scheme.

919 **3.4.1.5 Certificate Status Request**

920 *Applies to TLS versions: 1.0, 1.1, 1.2, 1.3*

921 When the client wishes to receive the revocation status of the TLS server certificate from the
922 TLS server, the client includes the Certificate Status Request (status_request) extension in the
923 ClientHello message. Upon receipt of the status_request extension, a server with a certificate
924 issued by a CA that supports OCSP **shall** include the certificate status along with its certificate
925 by sending a CertificateStatus message immediately following the Certificate message.[25] While
926 the extension itself is extensible, only OCSP-type certificate status is defined in [28]. This
927 extension is also called OCSP stapling.

928 ### 3.4.2 Conditional TLS Extensions

929 Support the use of the following TLS extensions under the circumstances described in the
930 following paragraphs:

931 1. The Fallback Signaling Cipher Suite Value (SCSV) **shall** be supported if the server
932 supports versions of TLS prior to TLS 1.2 and does not support TLS 1.3.
933 2. The Supported Groups extension **shall be** supported if the server supports ephemeral
934 ECDH cipher suites or if the server supports TLS 1.3.
935 3. The Key Share extension **shall be** supported if the server supports TLS 1.3.
936 4. The EC Point Format extension **shall** be supported if the server supports EC cipher
937 suites.
938 5. The Multiple Certificate Status extension **should** be supported if status information for
939 the server's certificate is available via OCSP, and the extension is supported by the server
940 implementation.
941 6. The Trusted CA Indication extension **shall** be supported if the server communicates with
942 memory-constrained clients (e.g., low-memory client devices in the Internet of Things),
943 and the server has been issued certificates by multiple CAs.
944 7. The Encrypt-then-MAC extension **shall** be supported if the server is configured to
945 negotiate CBC cipher suites.
946 8. The Truncated HMAC extension may be supported if the server communicates with
947 constrained device clients, cipher suites that use CBC mode are supported, and the server
948 implementation does not support variable-length padding.
949 9. The Pre-Shared Key extension may be supported if the server supports TLS 1.3.
950 10. The Pre-Shared Key Exchange Modes extension **shall** be supported if the server supports
951 TLS 1.3 and the Pre-Shared Key extension.
952 11. The Supported Versions extension **shall** be supported if the server supports TLS 1.3.
953 12. The Cookie extension **shall** be supported if the server supports TLS 1.3.
954 13. The Certificate Signature Algorithms Extension **shall** be supported if the server supports
955 TLS 1.3, and **should** be supported for TLS 1.2.
956 14. The Signed Certificate Timestamps extension **should** be supported if the server's
957 certificate was issued by a publicly trusted CA, and the certificate does not include a
958 Signed Certificate Timestamps List extension.

---

[25] In TLS 1.3 the server includes the certificate status in the Certificate message.

959   **3.4.2.1 Fallback Signaling Cipher Suite Value (SCSV)**

960   *Applies to TLS versions: 1.0, 1.1, 1.2*

961   TLS 1.3 includes a downgrade protection mechanism that previous versions do not. In versions
962   prior to TLS 1.3, an attacker can use an external version negotiation as a means to force
963   unnecessary protocol downgrades on a connection. In particular, the attacker can make it appear
964   that the connection failed with the requested TLS version, and some client implementations will
965   try the connection again with a downgraded protocol version. This cipher suite value, described
966   in RFC 7507 [41], provides a mechanism to prevent unintended protocol downgrades in versions
967   prior to TLS 1.3. Clients signal when a connection is a fallback, and if the server deems it
968   inappropriate (i.e., the server supports a higher TLS version), the server returns a fatal alert.

969   When TLS versions prior to TLS 1.2 are supported by the server, and TLS version 1.3 is not
970   supported, the fallback SCSV **shall** be supported.

971   **3.4.2.2 Supported Groups**

972   *Applies to TLS versions: 1.0, 1.1, 1.2, 1.3*

973   The Supported Groups extension (supported_groups) allows the client to indicate the domain
974   parameter groups that it supports to the server. The extension was originally called the Supported
975   Elliptic Curves extension (elliptic_curves), and was only used for elliptic curve groups, but it
976   may now also be used to negotiate finite field groups. In TLS 1.3, the Supported Groups
977   extension must be used to negotiate both elliptic curve and finite field groups. Servers that
978   support either ephemeral ECDH cipher suites or TLS 1.3 **shall** support this extension. When
979   elliptic curve cipher suites are configured, at least one of the NIST-approved curves, P-256
980   (secp256r1) and P-384 (secp384r1), **shall** be supported as described in RFC 8422 [44].
981   Additional NIST-recommended elliptic curves are listed in SP 800-56A, Appendix D [7]. Finite
982   field groups that are approved for TLS in SP 800-56A, Appendix D may be supported.

983   **3.4.2.3 Key Share**

984   *Applies to TLS version 1.3*

985   The Key Share extension is used in TLS 1.3 to send cryptographic parameters. Servers that
986   support TLS 1.3 **shall** support this extension as described in Section 4.2.7 of RFC 8446 [50].

987   **3.4.2.4 Supported Point Formats**

988   *Applies to TLS versions: 1.0, 1.1, 1.2*

989   Servers that support EC cipher suites with TLS 1.2 and below **shall** be able to process the
990   supported point format received in the ClientHello message by the client. The servers **shall**
991   process this extension in accordance with Section 5.1 of RFC 8422 [44].

992   Servers that support EC cipher suites **shall** also be able to send the supported EC point format in
993   the ServerHello message as described in Section 5.2 of RFC 8422 [44].

994   **3.4.2.5 Multiple Certificate Status**

995   *Applies to TLS versions: 1.0, 1.1, 1.2*

996   The multiple certificate status extension improves on the Certificate Status Request extension
997   described in Section 3.4.1.5 by allowing the client to request the status of all certificates provided
998   by the server in the TLS handshake. When the server returns the revocation status of all the
999   certificates in the server certificate chain, the client does not need to query any revocation service
1000   providers, such as OCSP responders. This extension is documented in RFC 6961 [47]. Servers
1001   that have this capability and that have certificates issued by CAs that support OCSP **should** be
1002   configured to support this extension.

1003   **3.4.2.6 Trusted CA Indication**

1004   *Applies to TLS versions: 1.0, 1.1, 1.2*

1005   The trusted CA indication (trusted_ca_keys) extension allows a client to specify which CA root
1006   keys it possesses. This is useful for sessions where the client is memory-constrained and
1007   possesses a small number of root CA keys. Servers that communicate with memory-constrained
1008   clients and that have been issued certificates by multiple CAs **shall** be able to process and
1009   respond to the trusted CA indication extension received in a ClientHello message as described in
1010   [28].

1011   **3.4.2.7 Encrypt-then-MAC**

1012   *Applies to TLS versions: 1.0, 1.1, 1.2*

1013   Several attacks on CBC cipher suites have been possible due to the MAC-then-encrypt order of
1014   operations used in TLS versions 1.0, 1.1, and 1.2. The Encrypt-then-MAC extension alters the
1015   order that the encryption and MAC operations are applied to the data. This is believed to provide
1016   stronger security, and mitigate or prevent several known attacks on CBC cipher suites. Servers
1017   that are configured to negotiate CBC cipher suites **shall** support this extension as described in
1018   [32].

1019   **3.4.2.8 Truncated HMAC**

1020   *Applies to TLS versions: 1.0, 1.1, 1.2*

1021   The Truncated HMAC extension allows a truncation of the HMAC output to 80 bits for use as a
1022   MAC tag. An 80-bit MAC tag complies with the recommendations in SP 800-107 [19], but
1023   reduces the security provided by the integrity algorithm. Because forging a MAC tag is an online
1024   attack, and the TLS session will terminate immediately when an invalid MAC tag is encountered,
1025   the risk introduced by using this extension is low. However, truncated MAC tags **shall not** be
1026   used in conjunction with variable-length padding, due to attacks described by Paterson et al.
1027   [46]. This extension is only applicable when cipher suites that use CBC modes are supported.

1028   **3.4.2.9 Pre-Shared Key**

1029   *Applies to TLS version 1.3*

1030   The Pre-Shared Key extension (pre_shared_key), available in TLS 1.3, is used to indicate the
1031   identity of the pre-shared key to be used for PSK key establishment. In TLS 1.3 pre-shared keys
1032   may either be established out-of-band, as in TLS 1.2 are below, or in a previous connection, in
1033   which case they are used for session resumption. Servers that support TLS 1.3 may be
1034   configured to support this extension in order to support session resumption or to support the use
1035   of pre-shared keys that are established out-of-band.

1036   **3.4.2.10 Pre-Shared Key Exchange Modes**

1037   *Applies to TLS version 1.3*

1038   A TLS 1.3 client must send the Pre-Shared Key Exchange Modes extension
1039   (psk_key_exchange_modes) if it sends the Pre-Shared Key extension. TLS 1.3 servers use the
1040   list of key exchange modes present in the extension to select an appropriate key exchange
1041   method. TLS servers that support TLS 1.3 and the Pre-Shared Key extension **shall** support this
1042   extension.

1043   **3.4.2.11 Supported Versions**

1044   *Applies to TLS version 1.3*

1045   The supported versions extension is sent in the ClientHello message to indicate which versions
1046   of TLS the client supports. A TLS 1.3 server **shall** be able to process this extension. When it is
1047   absent from the ClientHello message, the server **shall** use the version negotiation specified in
1048   TLS 1.2 and earlier.

1049   **3.4.2.12 Cookie**

1050   *Applies to TLS version 1.3*

1051   The cookie extension allows the server to force the client to prove that it is reachable at its
1052   apparent network address, and offload state information to the client. Servers that support TLS
1053   1.3 may support the cookie extension in accordance with RFC 8446 [50].

1054   **3.4.2.13 Certificate Signature Algorithms**

1055   *Applies to TLS versions: 1.2, 1.3*

1056   The Certificate Signature Algorithms extension (signature_algorithms_cert) indicates the
1057   signature algorithms that may be used in certificates. (When it is not present, algorithms in the
1058   Signature Algorithms extension apply to certificates as well.) TLS servers that support TLS 1.3
1059   **shall** support this extension, and it **should** be supported for TLS 1.2.

1060 **3.4.2.14 Signed Certificate Timestamps**

1061 *Applies to TLS versions: 1.0, 1.1, 1.2, 1.3*

1062 The Certificate Transparency project (described in RFC 6962 [39]) strives to reduce the impact
1063 of certificate-based threats by making the issuance of CA-signed certificates more transparent.
1064 This is done through the use of public logs of certificates, public log monitoring, and public
1065 certificate auditing. Certificate logs are cryptographically assured records of certificates that are
1066 open to public scrutiny. Certificates may be appended to logs, but they cannot be removed,
1067 modified, or inserted into the middle of a log. Monitors watch certificate logs for suspicious
1068 certificates, such as those that were not authorized by the domain they claim to represent.
1069 Auditors have the ability to check the membership of a particular certificate in a log, as well as
1070 verify the integrity and consistency of logs.

1071 Evidence that the server's certificate has been submitted to Certificate Transparency logs may be
1072 provided to clients either in the certificate itself or in a Signed Certificate Timestamps TLS
1073 extension (signed_certificate_timestamp). Servers with certificates issued by publicly trusted
1074 CAs that do not include a Signed Certificate Timestamps List extension **should** support the
1075 Signed Certificate Timestamps TLS extension.

1076 **3.4.3   Discouraged TLS Extensions**

1077 The following extensions **should not** be used:

1078   1. Client Certificate URL

1079   2. Early Data Indication

1080 The Raw Public Keys extension **shall not** be supported.

1081 **3.4.3.1   Client Certificate URL**

1082 *Applies to TLS versions: 1.0, 1.1, 1.2*

1083 The Client Certificate URL extension allows a client to send a URL pointing to a certificate,
1084 rather than sending a certificate to the server during mutual authentication. This can be very
1085 useful for mutual authentication with constrained clients. However, this extension can be used
1086 for malicious purposes. The URL could belong to an innocent server on which the client would
1087 like to perform a denial of service attack, turning the TLS server into an attacker. A server that
1088 supports this extension also acts as a client while retrieving a certificate, and therefore becomes
1089 subject to additional security concerns. For these reasons, the Client Certificate URL extension
1090 **should not** be supported. However, if an agency determines that the risks are minimal, and this
1091 extension is needed for environments where clients are in constrained devices, the extension may
1092 be supported. If the client certificate URL extension is supported, the server **shall** be configured
1093 to mitigate the security concerns described above and in Section 11.3 of [28].

1094 **3.4.3.2   Early Data Indication**

1095 *Applies to TLS version 1.3*

1096　The Early Data Indication extension (early_data) allows the client to send application data in the
1097　ClientHello message when pre-shared keys are used. This includes pre-shared keys that are
1098　established out-of-band, as well as those used for session resumption. TLS does not protect this
1099　early data against replay attacks. Servers **should not** process early data received in the
1100　ClientHello message. If the server is configured to send the Early Data Indication extension, the
1101　server **shall** use methods of replay protection, such as those described in Section 8 of RFC 8446
1102　[50]. See Section 3.6 for more information on early data (also called 0-RTT data).

1103　### 3.4.3.3　Raw Public Keys

1104　*Applies to TLS versions: 1.0, 1.1 1.2, 1.3*

1105　The Raw Public Keys extension, described in RFC 7250 [45], provides an alternative to
1106　certificate-based authentication that only uses the information contained in the
1107　SubjectPublicKeyInfo field an X.509 version 3 certificate. While this reduces the size of the
1108　public key structure and simplifies processing, it removes any assurances that a public key
1109　belongs to a particular entity. To provide authentication, an out-of-band binding between public
1110　key and entity must be used.

1111　### 3.5　Client Authentication

1112　Where strong cryptographic client authentication is required, TLS servers may use the TLS
1113　protocol client authentication option to request a certificate from the client to cryptographically
1114　authenticate the client.[26] For example, the Personal Identity Verification (PIV) Authentication
1115　certificate [64] (and the associated private key) provides a suitable option for strong
1116　authentication of Federal employees and contractors. To ensure that agencies are positioned to
1117　take full advantage of the PIV Card, all TLS servers that perform client authentication **shall**
1118　implement certificate-based client authentication.

1119　The client authentication option requires the server to implement the X.509 path validation
1120　mechanism and a trust anchor store. Requirements for these mechanisms are specified in
1121　Sections 3.5.1 and 3.5.2, respectively. To ensure that cryptographic authentication actually
1122　results in strong authentication, client keys **shall** contain at least 112 bits of security. Section
1123　3.5.3 describes mechanisms that can contribute, albeit indirectly, to enforcing this requirement.
1124　Section 3.5.4 describes the client's use of the server hints list.

1125　The TLS server **shall** be configurable to terminate the connection with a fatal "handshake
1126　failure" alert when a client certificate is requested, and the client does not have a suitable
1127　certificate.

---

[26] The CertificateVerify message is sent to explicitly verify a client certificate that has a signing capability. In TLS 1.1 (and TLS 1.0), this message uses SHA-1 to generate a signature on all handshake messages that came before it. SP 800-131A [10] states that the use of SHA-1 for digital signature generation is disallowed after 2013. Even if a collision is found, the client must use its private key to authenticate itself by signing the hash. Due to the client random and server random values, the server, the client, or a third party cannot use a colliding set of messages to masquerade as the client or server in future connections. Any modification to this message, preceding messages, or subsequent messages will ultimately result in a failed connection. Therefore, SHA-1 is allowed for generating digital signatures in the TLS CertificateVerify message.

1128   **3.5.1   Path Validation**

1129   The client certificate **shall** be validated in accordance with the certification path validation rules
1130   specified in Section 6 of [18]. In addition, the revocation status of each certificate in the
1131   certification path **shall** be validated using the Online Certificate Status Protocol (OCSP) or a
1132   certificate revocation list (CRL). OCSP checking **shall** be in compliance with RFC 6960 [55].

1133   Revocation information **shall** be obtained as described in Section 3.2.2.

1134   The server **shall** be able to determine the certificate policies that the client certificate is trusted
1135   for by using the certification path validation rules specified in Section 6 of [18]. Server and
1136   backend applications may use this determination to accept or reject the certificate. Checking
1137   certificate policies assures the server that only client certificates that have been issued with
1138   acceptable assurance, in terms of CA and registration system and process security, are accepted.

1139   Not all commercial products may support the public-key certification path validation and
1140   certificate policy processing rules listed and cited above. When implementing client
1141   authentication, the Federal agencies **shall** either use the commercial products that meet these
1142   requirements or augment commercial products to meet these requirements.

1143   The server **shall** be able to provide the client certificate, and the certificate policies for which the
1144   client certification path is valid, to the applications in order to support access control decisions.

1145   **3.5.2   Trust Anchor Store**

1146   Having an excessive number of trust anchors installed in the TLS application can expose the
1147   application to all the PKIs emanating from those trust anchors. The best way to minimize the
1148   exposure is to only include the trust anchors in the trust anchor store that are absolutely
1149   necessary for client public-key certificate authentication.

1150   The server **shall** be configured with only the trust anchors that the server trusts, and of those,
1151   only the ones that are required to authenticate the clients, in the case where the server supports
1152   client authentication in TLS. These trust anchors are typically a small subset of the trust anchors
1153   that may be included on the server by default. Also, note that this trust anchor store is distinct
1154   from the machine trust anchor store. Thus, the default set of trust anchors **shall** be examined to
1155   determine if any of them are required for client authentication. Some specific enterprise and/or
1156   PKI service provider trust anchor may need to be added.

1157   In the U.S. federal environment, in most situations, the Federal Common Policy Root or the
1158   agency root (if cross certified with the Federal Bridge Certification Authority or the Federal
1159   Common Policy Root) should be sufficient to build a certification path to the client certificates.

1160   System administrators of a TLS server that supports certificate-based client authentication **shall**
1161   perform an analysis of the client certificate issuers and use that information to determine the
1162   minimum set of trust anchors required for the server. The server **shall** be configured to only use
1163   those trust anchors.

1164　### 3.5.3　Checking the Client Key Size

1165　The only direct mechanism for a server to check whether the key size and algorithms presented
1166　in a client public-key certificate are acceptable is for the server to examine the public key and
1167　algorithm in the client's certificate. An indirect mechanism is to check that the certificate
1168　policies extension in the client public-key certificate indicates the minimum cryptographic
1169　strength of the signature and hashing algorithms used, and for the server to perform certificate
1170　policy processing and checking. The server **shall** check the client key length if client
1171　authentication is performed, and the server implementation provides a mechanism to do so.
1172　Federal Agencies **shall** use the key size guidelines provided in SP 800-131A [10] to check the
1173　client key size.

1174　### 3.5.4　Server Hints List

1175　Clients may use the list of trust anchors sent by the server in the CertificateRequest message to
1176　determine if the client's certification path terminates at one of these trust anchors. The list sent
1177　by the server is known as a "hints list." When the server and client are in different PKI domains,
1178　and the trust is established via direct cross-certification between the two PKI domains (i.e., the
1179　server PKI domain and the client PKI domain) or via transitive cross-certification (i.e., through
1180　cross-certifications among multiple PKI domains), the client may erroneously decide that its
1181　certificate will not be accepted by the server since the client's trust anchor is not sent in the hints
1182　list. To mitigate this failure, the server **shall** either 1) maintain the trust anchors of the various
1183　PKIs whose subscribers are the potential clients for the server, and include them in the hints list,
1184　or 2) be configured to send an empty hints list so that the client can always provide a certificate it
1185　possesses. The hints list **shall** be distinct from the server's trust anchor store.[27] In other words,
1186　the server **shall** continue to only populate its trust anchor store with the trust anchor of the
1187　server's PKI domain and the domains it needs to trust directly for client authentication. Note that
1188　the distinction between the server hints list and the server's own trust store is as follows: 1) the
1189　hints list is the list of trust anchors that a potential client might trust; and 2) the server's trust
1190　store is the list of trust anchors that the server explicitly trusts.

1191　### 3.6　Session Resumption and Early Data

1192　Previous TLS sessions can be resumed, allowing for a connection to be established using an
1193　abbreviated handshake. All versions of TLS offer session resumption, although the mechanism
1194　for performing resumption differs. A server may be configured to ignore requests to resume a
1195　session, if the implementation allows it.

1196　Additional mechanisms have been developed for session resumption, such as the Stateless TLS
1197　Session Resumption extension [54]. While these guidelines neither encourage or discourage the
1198　use of such mechanisms, it is important to understand the security impact if long term or shared
1199　keys are compromised. If resumption is allowed, frequent key rotation and short lifetimes for
1200　resumption information are recommended, as applicable. See [58] for discussion on the security

---

[27] Depending on the server and client trust anchors, the two lists could be identical, could have some trust anchors in common, or
have no trust anchors in common.

1201   impacts of resumption mechanisms.

1202   TLS 1.3 allows the client to send data in the first flight of handshake, known as 0-RTT data. This
1203   practice may provide opportunities for attackers, such as replay attacks.[28] The TLS 1.3
1204   specification describes two mechanisms to mitigate threats introduced by 0-RTT data. One of
1205   these mechanisms is single-use tickets, which allows each session ticket to be used only once. It
1206   may be difficult to implement this mechanism in an environment with distributed servers, as a
1207   session database must be shared between servers. ClientHello recording is a second mechanism
1208   that defends against replay attacks by recording a unique value derived from the ClientHello and
1209   rejecting duplicates. To limit the size of the list, the server can maintain a list only within a
1210   specified time window. In general, 0-RTT data **should not** be accepted by the server. If the
1211   server does allow 0-RTT data, then the server **should** use the single-use ticket mechanism in
1212   accordance with RFC 8446 (see Section 8 of [50]).

1213   **3.7   Compression Methods**

1214   The use of compression may enable attackers to perform attacks using compression-based side
1215   channels (e.g., [52], [11]). To defend against these attacks, the null compression method **shall** be
1216   enabled, and all other compression methods **shall** be disabled.

1217   **3.8   Operational Considerations**

1218   The sections above specify TLS-specific functionality. This functionality is necessary, but is not
1219   sufficient, to achieve security in an operational environment.

1220   Federal agencies **shall** ensure that TLS servers include appropriate network security protections
1221   as specified in other NIST guidelines, such as SP 800-53 [34].

1222   The server **shall** operate on a secure operating system.[29] Where the server relies on a FIPS 140
1223   Level 1 cryptographic module, the software and private key **shall** be protected using the
1224   operating system identification, authentication and access control mechanisms. In some highly
1225   sensitive applications, server private keys may require protection using a FIPS 140 Level 2 or
1226   higher hardware cryptographic module.

1227   The server and associated platform **shall** be kept up-to-date in terms of security patches. This is
1228   critical to various aspects of security.

1229

---

[28] TLS does not inherently provide replay protection for 0-RTT data.

[29] A secure operating system contains and uses the following features: operating system protection from applications and
    processes; operating system mediated isolation among applications and processes; user identification and authentication;
    access control based on authenticated user identity, and event logging of security-relevant activities.

1230 **4   Minimum Requirements for TLS Clients**

1231 This section provides a minimum set of requirements that a TLS client must meet in order to
1232 adhere to these guidelines. Requirements are organized as follows: TLS protocol version
1233 support; client keys and certificates; cryptographic support; TLS extension support; server
1234 authentication; session resumption; compression methods; and operational considerations.

1235 Specific requirements are stated as either implementation requirements or configuration
1236 requirements. Implementation requirements indicate that Federal agencies **shall not** procure TLS
1237 client implementations unless they include the required functionality. Configuration
1238 requirements indicate that system administrators are required to verify that particular features are
1239 enabled, or in some cases, configured appropriately if present.

4.1   Protocol Version Support

1241 The client **shall** be configured to use TLS 1.2 and **should** be configured to use TLS 1.3. The
1242 client may be configured to use TLS 1.1 and TLS 1.0 to facilitate communication with private
1243 sector servers. The client **shall not** be configured to use SSL 2.0 or SSL 3.0. Agencies **shall**
1244 support TLS 1.3 by January 1, 2024. After this date clients **shall** be configured to use TLS 1.3.
1245 Note that TLS 1.3 and 1.2 are intended to coexist, and should both be enabled after the TLS 1.3
1246 adoption deadline.

4.2   Client Keys and Certificates

1248 Some applications may require client authentication. For TLS, this can be achieved by
1249 performing mutual authentication using certificates.

4.2.1   Client Certificate Profile

1251 When certificate-based client authentication is needed, the client **shall** be configured with a
1252 certificate that adheres to the recommendations presented in this section. A client certificate may
1253 be configured on the system or located on an external device (e.g., a PIV Card). For this
1254 specification, the TLS client certificate **shall** be an X.509 version 3 certificate; both the public
1255 key contained in the certificate and the signature **shall** provide at least 112 bits of security. If the
1256 client supports TLS versions prior to TLS 1.2, the certificate **should** be signed with an algorithm
1257 that is consistent with the public key:[30]

1258 • Certificates containing RSA (signature), ECDSA, or DSA public keys **should** be signed
1259   with those same signature algorithms, respectively;
1260 • Certificates containing Diffie-Hellman certificates **should** be signed with DSA; and
1261 • Certificates containing ECDH public keys **should** be signed with ECDSA.

1262 The client certificate profile is listed in Table 4-1. In the absence of an agency-specific client
1263 certificate profile, this profile **should** be used for client certificates.

---

[30] This recommendation is an artifact of requirements in TLS 1.0 and 1.1.

1264   **Table 4-1: TLS Client Certificate Profile**

Field	Critical	Value	Description
Version	N/A	2	Version 3
Serial Number	N/A	Unique positive integer	Must be unique
Issuer Signature Algorithm	N/A	*Values by CA key type:*	
		sha256WithRSAEncryption {1 2 840 113549 1 1 11}, or stronger	CA with RSA key
		id-RSASSA-PSS { 1 2 840 113549 1 1 10 }	CA with RSA key
		ecdsa-with-SHA256 {1 2 840 10045 4 3 2}, or stronger	CA with elliptic curve key
		id-dsa-with-sha256 {2 16 840 1 101 3 4 3 2}, or stronger	CA with DSA key
Issuer Distinguished Name	N/A	Unique X.500 Issuing CA DN	A single value **shall** be encoded in each RDN. All attributes that are of directoryString type **shall** be encoded as a printable string.
Validity Period	N/A	3 years or less	Dates through 2049 expressed in UTCTime
Subject Distinguished Name	N/A	Unique X.500 subject DN per agency requirements	A single value **shall** be encoded in each RDN. All attributes that are of directoryString type **shall** be encoded as a printable string.
Subject Public Key Information	N/A	*Values by certificate type:*	
		rsaEncryption {1 2 840 113549 1 1 1}	RSA signature certificate 2048-bit RSA key modulus, or other approved lengths as defined in [FIPS186-4] and [5] Parameters: NULL
		ecPublicKey {1 2 840 10045 2 1}	ECDSA signature certificate or ECDH certificate Parameters: namedCurve OID for names curve specified in SP 800-186.[31] The curve **shall** be P-256 or P-384 SubjectPublic Key: Uncompressed EC Point.
		id-dsa {1 2 840 10040 4 1}	DSA signature certificate Parameters: p, q, g
		dhpublicnumber {1 2 840 10046 2 1}	DH certificate Parameters: p, g, q
Issuer's Signature	N/A	Same value as in Issuer Signature Algorithm	
Extensions			
Authority Key Identifier	No	Octet String	Same as subject key identifier in issuing CA certificate

---

[31] The recommended elliptic curves now listed in FIPS 186-4 [62] will be moved to SP 800-186. Until SP 800-186 is published, the recommended elliptic curves should be taken from FIPS 186-4.

Field	Critical	Value	Description
			Prohibited: Issuer DN, Serial Number tuple
Subject Key Identifier	No	Octet String	Same as in PKCS-10 request or calculated by the issuing CA
Key Usage	Yes	digitalSignature	RSA certificate, DSA certificate, ECDSA certificate
		keyAgreement	ECDH certificate, DH certificate
Extended Key Usage	No	id-kp-clientAuth {1 3 6 1 5 5 7 3 2}	Required
		anyExtendedKeyUsage {2 5 29 37 0}	The anyExtendedKeyUsage OID **should** be present if the extended key usage extension is included, but there is no intention to limit the types of applications with which the certificate may be used (e.g., the certificate is a general-purpose authentication certificate).
			Prohibited: all others unless consistent with key usage extension
Certificate Policies	No	Per issuer's X.509 certificate policy	
Subject Alternative Name	No	RFC 822 e-mail address, Universal Principal Name (UPN), DNS Name, and/or others	Optional
Authority Information Access	No	id-ad-caIssuers	Required. Access method entry contains HTTP URL for certificates issued to issuing CA
		id-ad-ocsp	Optional. Access method entry contains HTTP URL for the issuing CA OCSP responder
CRL Distribution Points	No	See comments	Optional: HTTP value in distributionPoint field pointing to a full and complete CRL. Prohibited: reasons and cRLIssuer fields, and nameRelativetoCRLIssuer CHOICE

1265

1266 If a client has multiple certificates that meet the requirements of the TLS server, the TLS client
1267 (e.g., a browser) may ask the user to select from a list of certificates. The extended key usage
1268 (EKU) extension limits the operations for which the keys in a certificate may be used, and so the
1269 use of the EKU extension in client certificates may eliminate this request. If the EKU extension
1270 is included in client certificates, then the id-kp-client-auth key purpose OID **should** be included
1271 in the certificates to be used for TLS client authentication and **should** be omitted from any other
1272 certificates.

1273 Client certificates are also filtered by TLS clients on the basis of an ability to build a path to one
1274 of the trust anchors in the hints list sent by the server, as described in Section 3.5.4.

1275 **4.2.2   Obtaining Revocation Status Information for the Server Certificate**

1276 The client **shall** perform revocation checking of the server certificate. Revocation information
1277 can be obtained by the client from one of the following locations:

1278   1. OCSP response or responses in the server's CertificateStatus message ([28], [47]) (or
1279   Certificate message in TLS 1.3);

1280   2. Certificate Revocation List (CRL) or OCSP response in the client's local certificate store;

1281   3. OCSP response from a locally configured OCSP responder;

1282   4. OCSP response from the OCSP responder location identified in the OCSP field in the
1283   Authority Information Access extension in the server certificate; or

1284   5. CRL from the CRL Distribution Point extension in the server certificate.

1285 When the server does not provide the revocation status, the local certificate store does not have
1286 the current or a cogent CRL or OCSP response, and the OCSP responder and the CRL
1287 distribution point are unavailable or inaccessible at the time of TLS session establishment, the
1288 client will either terminate the connection or accept a potentially revoked or compromised
1289 certificate. The decision to accept or reject a certificate in this situation **should** be made
1290 according to agency policy.

1291 Other emerging concepts that can be useful in lieu of revocation checking are further discussed
1292 in Appendix E.2.

1293 4.2.3 Client Public-Key Certificate Assurance

1294 The client public-key certificate may be trusted by the servers on the basis of the policies,
1295 procedures and security controls used to issue the client public-key certificate as described in
1296 Section 3.5.1. For example, these guidelines recommend that the PIV Authentication certificate
1297 be the norm for authentication of Federal employees and long-term contractors. PIV
1298 Authentication certificate policy is defined in the Federal PKI Common Policy Framework [30],
1299 and PIV-I Authentication certificate policy is defined in the X.509 Certificate Policy for the
1300 Federal Bridge Certification Authority [59]. Depending on the requirements of the server-side
1301 application, other certificate policies may also be acceptable. Guidance regarding other
1302 certificate policies is outside the scope of these guidelines.

1303 4.3 Cryptographic Support

1304 4.3.1 Cipher Suites

1305 The acceptable cipher suites for a TLS client are the same as those for a TLS server. General-
1306 purpose cipher suites are listed in Section 3.3.1. Cipher suites appropriate for pre-shared key
1307 environments for TLS 1.2 and prior versions are listed in Appendix C. Applications that require
1308 RSA key transport as the key exchange may use cipher suites listed in Appendix D during the
1309 deprecation period. When ephemeral keys are used to establish the master secret, each ephemeral
1310 key-pair (i.e., the server ephemeral key-pair and the client ephemeral key-pair) **shall** have at least
1311 112 bits of security.

1312 The client **should not** be configured to use cipher suites other than those listed in Section 3.3.1,
1313 Appendix C, or Appendix D.

1314 To mitigate attacks against CBC mode, TLS implementations that support versions prior to TLS
1315 1.3 **shall** use the bad_record_mac error to indicate a padding error. Implementations **shall**
1316 compute the MAC regardless of whether padding errors exist. TLS implementations **should**
1317 support constant-time decryption, or near constant-time decryption. This does not apply to TLS

1318   1.3 implementations, as they do not support cipher suites that use CBC mode.

4.3.2   Validated Cryptography

1320   The client **shall** use validated cryptography, as described for the server in Section 3.3.3.

1321   The validated random number generator **shall** be used to generate the random bytes (32 bytes in
1322   TLS 1.3; 28 bytes in prior TLS versions) of the client random value. The validated random
1323   number generator **should** be used to generate the 4-byte timestamp of the client random value for
1324   TLS versions prior to TLS 1.3.

4.4   TLS Extension Support

1326   In general, it is advised that clients only be configured to support extensions that are required for
1327   interoperability or enhance security. Extensions that are not needed **should not** be enabled.

4.4.1   Mandatory TLS Extensions

1329   The client **shall** be configured to use the following extensions:

1330   1. Renegotiation Indication
1331   2. Server Name Indication
1332   3. Extended Master Secret
1333   4. Signature Algorithms
1334   5. Certificate Status Request

4.4.1.1   Renegotiation Indication

1336   *Applies to TLS versions: 1.0, 1.1, 1.2*

1337   The Renegotiation Indication extension is required by these guidelines as described in Section
1338   3.4.1.1. Clients **shall** perform the initial and subsequent renegotiations in accordance with RFC
1339   5746 [51].

4.4.1.2   Server Name Indication

1341   *Applies to TLS versions: 1.0, 1.1, 1.2, 1.3*

1342   The server name indication extension is described in Section 3.4.1.2. The client **shall** be capable
1343   of including this extension in a ClientHello message, as described in RFC 6066 [28].

4.4.1.3   Extended Master Secret

1345   *Applies to TLS versions: 1.0, 1.1, 1.2*

1346   The Extended Master Secret extension, described in Section 3.4.1.3, prevents man-in-the-middle
1347   attacks by binding the master secret to a hashed log of the full handshake. The client **shall**
1348   support this extension.

1349 **4.4.1.4 Signature Algorithms**

1350 *Applies to TLS versions: 1.2, 1.3*

1351 The clients **shall** assert acceptable hashing and signature algorithm pairs in this extension in TLS
1352 1.2 and TLS 1.3 ClientHello messages. The extension, its syntax, and processing rules are
1353 described in Sections 7.4.1.4.1, 7.4.4, 7.4.6 and 7.4.8 of RFC 5246 [24] and in Section 4.2.3 of
1354 RFC 8446 [50]. Note that the extension described in RFC 8446 updates the extension described
1355 in RFC 5246 by adding an additional signature scheme.

1356 **4.4.1.5 Certificate Status Request**

1357 *Applies to TLS versions: 1.0, 1.1, 1.2, 1.3*

1358 The client **shall** include the "status_request" extension in the ClientHello message.

1359 **4.4.2 Conditional TLS Extensions**

1360 A TLS client supports the following TLS extensions under the circumstances described:

1361   1. The Fallback Signaling Cipher Suite Value (SCSV) **shall** be supported if the client
1362   supports versions of TLS prior to TLS 1.2 and does not support TLS 1.3.
1363   2. The Supported Groups extension **shall** be supported if the client supports ephemeral
1364   ECDH cipher suites or if the client supports TLS 1.3.
1365   3. The Key Share extension **shall be** supported if the client supports TLS 1.3.
1366   4. The EC Point Format TLS extension **shall** be supported if the client supports EC cipher
1367   suite(s).
1368   5. The Multiple Certificate Status extension **should** be enabled if the extension is supported
1369   by the client implementation.
1370   6. The Trusted CA Indication extension **should** be supported by clients that run on memory-
1371   constrained devices where only a small number of CA root keys are stored.
1372   7. The Encrypt-then-MAC extension **shall** be supported when CBC mode cipher suites are
1373   configured.
1374   8. The Truncated HMAC extension may be supported by clients that run on constrained
1375   devices when variable-length padding is not supported and cipher suites that use CBC
1376   mode are supported.
1377   9. The Pre-Shared Key extension may be supported by TLS 1.3 clients.
1378   10. The Pre-Shared Key Exchange Modes extension **shall** be supported by TLS 1.3 clients
1379   that support the Pre-Shared Key extension.
1380   11. The Supported Versions extension **shall** be supported by TLS 1.3 clients.
1381   12. The Cookie extension **shall** be supported by TLS 1.3 clients.
1382   13. The Certificate Signature Algorithms Extension **shall** be supported if the client supports
1383   TLS 1.3, and **should** be supported for TLS 1.2.

1384 **4.4.2.1 Fallback Signaling Cipher Suite Value (SCSV)**

1385 *Applies to TLS versions: 1.0, 1.1, 1.2*

1386   This cipher suite value, described in Section 3.4.2.1, provides a mechanism to prevent
1387   unintended protocol downgrades in TLS versions prior to TLS 1.3. Clients signal when a
1388   connection is a fallback, and if the server supports a higher TLS version, the server returns a fatal
1389   alert. If the client does not support TLS 1.3, and is attempting to connect with a TLS version
1390   prior to TLS 1.2, the client **shall** include TLS_FALLBACK_SCSV at the end of the cipher suite
1391   list in the ClientHello message.

1392   **4.4.2.2   Supported Groups**

1393   *Applies to TLS versions: 1.0, 1.1, 1.2, 1.3*

1394   The Supported Groups extension (supported_groups) is described in Section 3.4.2.2. Client
1395   implementations **shall** send this extension in TLS 1.3 ClientHello messages and in ClientHello
1396   messages that include ephemeral ECDH cipher suites. When elliptic curve cipher suites are
1397   configured, at least one of the NIST-approved curves, P-256 (secp256r1) and P-384 (secp384r1),
1398   **shall** be supported as described in RFC 8422 [44]. Additional NIST-recommended elliptic
1399   curves are listed in SP 800-56A, Appendix D [7]. Finite field groups that are approved for TLS
1400   in SP 800-56A, Appendix D may be supported.

1401   **4.4.2.3   Key Share**

1402   *Applies to TLS version 1.3*

1403   The Key Share extension is used to send cryptographic parameters. Clients that support TLS 1.3
1404   **shall** support this extension as described in Section 4.2.7 of RFC 8446 [50].

1405   **4.4.2.4   Supported Point Formats**

1406   *Applies to TLS versions: 1.0, 1.1, 1.2*

1407   The clients that support EC cipher suites with TLS 1.2 and below **shall** be capable of specifying
1408   supported point formats in the ClientHello message, in accordance with Section 5.1 of [44].

1409   Clients that support EC cipher suites **shall** support the processing of at least one[32] of the EC
1410   point formats received in the ServerHello message, as described in Section 5.2 of [44].

1411   **4.4.2.5   Multiple Certificate Status**

1412   *Applies to TLS versions: 1.0, 1.1, 1.2*

1413   The multiple certificate status extension is described in Section 3.4.2.5. This extension improves
1414   on the Certificate Status Request extension described in Section 3.4.1.5 by allowing the client to
1415   request the status of all certificates provided by the server in the TLS handshake. This extension
1416   is documented in RFC 6961 [47]. Client implementations that have this capability **should** be

---

[32] The uncompressed point format must be supported, and all others are deprecated in TLS, as described in Sections 5.1.2 of RFC 8422 [44].

1417   configured to include this extension in the ClientHello message.

4.4.2.6 Trusted CA Indication

1419   *Applies to TLS versions: 1.0, 1.1, 1.2*

1420   Clients that run on memory-constrained devices where only a small number of CA root keys are
1421   stored **should** be capable of including the trusted CA indication (trusted_ca_keys) extension in a
1422   ClientHello message as described in [28].

4.4.2.7 Encrypt-then-MAC

1424   *Applies to TLS versions: 1.0, 1.1, 1.2*

1425   The Encrypt-then-MAC extension, described in Section 3.4.2.7, can mitigate or prevent several
1426   known attacks on CBC cipher suites. In order for this modified order of operations to be applied,
1427   both server and client need to implement the Encrypt-then-MAC extension and negotiate its use.
1428   When CBC mode cipher suites are configured, clients **shall** support this extension as described
1429   in RFC 7366 [32]. The client **shall** include this extension in the ClientHello message whenever
1430   the ClientHello message includes CBC cipher suites.

4.4.2.8 Truncated HMAC

1432   *Applies to TLS versions: 1.0, 1.1, 1.2*

1433   The Truncated HMAC extension is described in Section 3.4.2.8. Clients running on constrained
1434   devices may support this extension. The Truncated HMAC extension **shall not** be used in
1435   conjunction with variable-length padding, due to attacks described by Paterson et al. [46]. This
1436   extension is only applicable when cipher suites that use CBC modes are supported.

4.4.2.9 Pre-Shared Key

1438   *Applies to TLS version 1.3*

1439   The Pre-Shared Key extension (pre_shared_key) is used to indicate the identity of the pre-shared
1440   key to be used for PSK key establishment. In TLS 1.3 pre-shared keys may either be established
1441   out-of-band, as in TLS 1.2 and prior versions, or in a previous connection, in which case they are
1442   used for session resumption. Clients that support TLS 1.3 may be configured to use this
1443   extension in order to allow session resumption or to allow the use of pre-shared keys that are
1444   established out-of-band.

4.4.2.10 Pre-Shared Key Exchange Modes

1446   *Applies to TLS version 1.3*

1447   A TLS 1.3 client must send the Pre-Shared Key Exchange Modes extension
1448   (psk_key_exchange_modes) if it sends the Pre-Shared Key extension, otherwise the server will
1449   abort the handshake. TLS clients that support TLS 1.3 and the Pre-Shared Key extension **shall**
1450   implement this extension.

1451   **4.4.2.11 Supported Versions**

1452   *Applies to TLS version 1.3*

1453   The supported versions extension indicates which versions of TLS the client is able to negotiate.
1454   A TLS 1.3 client **shall** send this extension in the ClientHello message.

1455   **4.4.2.12 Cookie**

1456   *Applies to TLS version 1.3*

1457   The cookie extension allows the server to force the client to prove that it is reachable at its
1458   apparent network address, and offload state to the client. Clients that support TLS 1.3 **shall**
1459   support the cookie extension in accordance with RFC 8446 [50].

1460   **4.4.2.13 Certificate Signature Algorithms**

1461   *Applies to TLS versions: 1.2, 1.3*

1462   The Certificate Signature Algorithms extension (signature_algorithms_cert) indicates the
1463   signature algorithms that may be used in certificates. This allows the entity requesting a
1464   certificate (client or server) to request different signature algorithms for the certificate than for
1465   the TLS handshake. A client may send this extension to the server, and may receive this
1466   extension from a server that is requesting certificate-based client authentication. This extension
1467   does not need to be sent if the algorithms in the Signature Algorithms extension apply to
1468   certificates as well. TLS client implementations that support TLS 1.3 **shall** support this
1469   extension, and it **should** be supported for TLS 1.2.

1470   **4.4.3   Discouraged TLS Extension**

1471   The following extensions **should not** be used:

1472   1. Client Certificate URL

1473   2. Early Data Indication

1474   The Raw Public Key extension **shall not** be supported.

1475   The reasons for discouraging the use of these extensions can be found in Section 3.4.3.

1476   **4.5   Server Authentication**

1477   The client **shall** be able to build the certification path for the server certificate presented in the
1478   TLS handshake with at least one of the trust anchors in the client trust store, if an appropriate
1479   trust anchor is present in the store. The client may use all or a subset of the following resources
1480   to build the certification path: the local certificate store, certificates received from the server
1481   during the handshake, LDAP, the resources declared in CA Repository field of the Subject
1482   Information Access extension in various CA certificates, and the resources declared in the CA
1483   Issuers field of the Authority Information Access extension in various certificates.

1484 **4.5.1   Path Validation**

1485   The client **shall** validate the server certificate in accordance with the certification path validation
1486   rules specified in Section 6 of [18]. The revocation status of each certificate in the certification
1487   path **shall** be checked using the Online Certificate Status Protocol (OCSP) or a certificate
1488   revocation list (CRL). OCSP checking **shall** be in compliance with [55]. Revocation information
1489   **shall** be obtained as described in Section 4.2.2.

1490   Not all clients support name constraint checking. Federal agencies **should** only procure clients
1491   that perform name constraint checking in order to obtain assurance that unauthorized certificates
1492   are properly rejected. As an alternative, a federal agency may procure clients that use one or
1493   more of the features discussed in Appendix E.1.

1494   The client **shall** terminate the TLS connection if path validation fails.

1495   Federal agencies **shall** only use clients that check that the DNS name or IP address, whichever is
1496   presented in the client TLS request, matches a DNS name or IP address contained in the server
1497   certificate. The client **shall** terminate the TLS connection if the name check fails.

1498 **4.5.2   Trust Anchor Store**

1499   Having an excessive number of trust anchors installed in the TLS client can increase the chances
1500   for the client to be spoofed. As the number of trust anchors increase, the number of CAs that the
1501   client trusts increases, and the chances that one of these CAs or its registration system or process
1502   will be compromised to issue TLS server certificates also increases.

1503   Clients **shall not** overpopulate their trust stores with various CA certificates that can be verified
1504   via cross-certification. Direct trust of these certificates can expose the clients unduly to a variety
1505   of situations, including but not limited to, revocation or compromise of these trust anchors.
1506   Direct trust also increases the operational and security burden on the clients to promulgate the
1507   addition and deletion of trust anchors. Instead, the client **shall** rely on the server overpopulating
1508   or not providing the hints list to mitigate the client certificate selection and path-building
1509   problem as discussed in Section 3.5.4.

1510 **4.5.3   Checking the Server Key Size**

1511   The only direct mechanism for a client to check if the key size presented in a server public
1512   certificate is acceptable is for the client to examine the server public key in the certificate. An
1513   indirect mechanism is to ensure that the server public-key certificate was issued under a policy
1514   that indicates the minimum cryptographic strength of the signature and hashing algorithms used.
1515   In some cases, this can be done by the client performing certificate policy processing and
1516   checking. However, since many TLS clients cannot be configured to accept or reject certificates
1517   based on the policies under which they were issued, this may require ensuring that the trust
1518   anchor store only contains CAs that issue certificates under acceptable policies. The client **shall**
1519   check the server public key length if the client implementation provides a mechanism to do so.
1520   The client **shall** also check the server public key length if the server uses ephemeral keys for the
1521   creation of the master secret, and the client implementation provides a mechanism to do so.

1522   The length of each write key is determined by the negotiated cipher suite. Restrictions on the
1523   length of the shared session keys can be enforced by configuring the client to only support cipher
1524   suites that meet the key length requirements.

4.5.4   User Interface

1526   When the TLS client is a browser, the browser interface can be used to determine if a TLS
1527   session is in effect. The indication that a TLS session is in effect varies by browser. Examples of
1528   indicators include a padlock in the URL bar, the word "secure" preceding the URL, or a different
1529   color for the URL bar. Some clients, such as browsers, may allow further investigation of the
1530   server certificate and negotiated session parameters by clicking on the lock (or other indicator).
1531   Users **should** examine the interface for the presence of the indicator to ensure that the TLS
1532   session is in force and **should** also visually examine web site URLs to ensure that the user
1533   intended to visit the indicated web site. Users **should** be aware that URLs can appear to be
1534   legitimate, but still not be valid. For example, the numeric "1" and the letter "l" appear quite
1535   similar or the same to the human eye.

1536   Client authentication keys may be located outside of the client (e.g., PIV Cards). Users **shall**
1537   follow the relevant policies and procedures for protecting client authentication keys outside of
1538   the client.

4.6   Session Resumption and Early Data

1540   Session resumption considerations and server recommendations were given in Section 3.6. There
1541   are no specific recommendations for clients regarding session resumption when using TLS 1.2,
1542   1.1, or 1.0. Clients typically will not know if any anti-replay mechanisms are in place to prevent
1543   replay attacks on 0-RTT data in TLS 1.3. Therefore, clients using TLS 1.3 **should not** send 0-
1544   RTT data.

1545   RFC 7918 [38] describes a technique, called False Start, that allows a TLS 1.2 client to send
1546   early data. While this concept is similar to the 0-RTT data of TLS 1.3, there are differences that
1547   affect security. For example, an attacker may perform downgrade attacks, both of protocol
1548   versions and cipher suites, and obtain client data before the handshake is determined to be
1549   invalid. While RFC 7918 provides recommendations for improving security, it is safest to
1550   disable False Start unless there is a real need for it. TLS 1.2 clients **shall not** use False Start.

4.7   Compression Methods

1552   The client **shall** follow the same compression recommendations as the server, which are
1553   described in Section 3.7.

4.8   Operational Considerations

1555   The client and associated platform **shall** be kept up-to-date in terms of security patches. This is
1556   critical to various aspects of security.

1557   Once the TLS-protected data is received at the client, and decrypted and authenticated by the
1558   TLS layer of the client system, the unencrypted data is available to the applications on the client

1559   platform.

1560   These guidelines do not mitigate the threats against the misuse or exposure of the client
1561   credentials that resides on the client machine. These credentials could contain the private key
1562   used for client authentication or other credentials (e.g., a one-time password (OTP) or user ID
1563   and password) for authenticating to a server-side application.

1564   For these reasons, the use of TLS does not obviate the need for the client to use appropriate
1565   security measures, as described in applicable Federal Information Processing Standards and
1566   NIST Special Publications, to protect computer systems and applications. Users **shall** operate
1567   client systems in accordance with agency and administrator instructions.

1568

1569   **Appendix A—Acronyms**

1570   Selected acronyms and abbreviations used in this paper are defined below.

3DES	Triple Data Encryption Algorithm (TDEA)
AEAD	Authenticated Encryption with Associated Data
AES	Advanced Encryption Standard
CA	Certification Authority
CBC	Cipher Block Chaining
CCM	Counter with CBC-MAC
CRL	Certificate Revocation List
DES	Data Encryption Standard
DH	Diffie-Hellman key exchange
DHE	Ephemeral Diffie-Hellman key exchange
DNS	Domain Name System
DNSSEC	DNS Security Extensions
DSA	Digital Signature Algorithm
DSS	Digital Signature Standard (implies DSA)
EC	Elliptic Curve
ECDHE	Ephemeral Elliptic Curve Diffie-Hellman
ECDSA	Elliptic Curve Digital Signature Algorithm
FIPS	Federal Information Processing Standard
GCM	Galois Counter Mode
HKDF	HMAC-based Extract-and-Expand Key Derivation Function
HMAC	Keyed-hash Message Authentication Code
IETF	Internet Engineering Task Force
KDF	Key derivation function
MAC	Message Authentication Code
OCSP	Online Certificate Status Protocol
OID	Object Identifier
PIV	Personal Identity Verification
PKI	Public Key Infrastructure
PRF	Pseudo-random Function
PSK	Pre-Shared Key

RFC	Request for Comments
SHA	Secure Hash Algorithm
SSL	Secure Sockets Layer
TLS	Transport Layer Security
URL	Uniform Resource Locator

1571

1572 **Appendix B—Interpreting Cipher Suite Names**

1573 TLS cipher suite names consist of a set of mnemonics separated by underscores (i.e., "_"). The
1574 naming convention in TLS 1.3 differs from the convention shared in TLS 1.0, 1.1, and 1.2.
1575 Section B.1 provides guidance for interpreting the names of cipher suites that are recommended
1576 in these guidelines for TLS versions 1.0, 1.1, and 1.2. Section B.2 provides guidance for
1577 interpreting the names of cipher suites for TLS 1.3. In all TLS cipher suites, the first mnemonic
1578 is the protocol name, i.e., "TLS".

1579 **B.1   Interpreting Cipher Suites Names in TLS 1.0, 1.1, and 1.2**

1580 As shown in Section 3.3.1, these cipher suites have the following form:

1581   TLS_*KeyExchangeAlg*_WITH_*EncryptionAlg*_*MessageAuthenticationAlg*

1582 *KeyExchangeAlg* consists of one or two mnemonics.

1583 • If there is only one mnemonic, it must be PSK, based on the recommendations in these
1584   guidelines. The single mnemonic PSK indicates that the premaster secret is established
1585   using only symmetric algorithms with pre-shared keys, as described in RFC 4279 [29].
1586   Pre-shared key cipher suites that are approved for use with TLS 1.2 are listed in
1587   Appendix C.
1588 • If there are two mnemonics following the protocol name, the first key exchange
1589   mnemonic should be DH, ECDH, DHE, or ECDHE.
1590   o When the first key exchange mnemonic is DH or ECDH, it indicates that the
1591   server's public key in its certificate is for either DH or ECDH key exchange, and
1592   the second mnemonic indicates the signature algorithm that was used by the
1593   issuing CA to sign the server certificate.
1594   o When the first key exchange mnemonic is DHE or ECDHE, it indicates that
1595   ephemeral DH or ECDH will be used for key exchange, with the second
1596   mnemonic indicating the server signature public key type that will be used to
1597   authenticate the server's ephemeral public key.[33]

1598 *EncryptionAlg* indicates the symmetric encryption algorithm and associated mode of operations.

1599 *MessageAuthenticationAlg* is generally the hashing algorithm to be used for HMAC, if
1600 applicable.[34] In cases where HMAC is not applicable (e.g., AES-GCM), or the cipher suite was
1601 defined after the release of the TLS 1.2 RFC, this mnemonic represents the hashing algorithm
1602 used with the PRF.

1603 The following examples illustrate how to interpret the cipher suite names:

---

[33] In this case, the signature algorithm used by the CA to sign the certificate is not articulated in the cipher suite.

[34] HMAC is not applicable when the symmetric encryption mode of operation is authenticated encryption. Note that the CCM
mode cipher suites do not specify the last mnemonic and require that SHA-256 be used for the PRF.

1604   • TLS_DHE_RSA_WITH_AES_256_CBC_SHA256: Ephemeral DH is used for the key
1605   exchange. The server's ephemeral public key is authenticated using the server's RSA
1606   public key. Once the handshake is completed, the messages are encrypted using AES-256
1607   in CBC mode. SHA-256 is used for both the PRF and HMAC computations.

1608   • TLS_ECDHE_ECDSA_WITH_AES_256_GCM_SHA384: Ephemeral ECDH is used for
1609   key exchange. The server's ephemeral public key is authenticated using the server's
1610   ECDSA public key. Once the handshake is completed, the messages are encrypted and
1611   authenticated using AES-256 in GCM mode, and SHA-384 is used for the PRF. Since an
1612   authenticated encryption mode is used, messages neither have nor require an HMAC
1613   message authentication code.

B.2   Interpreting Cipher Suites Names in TLS 1.3

1615   As shown in Section 3.3.1, these cipher suites have the following form:

1616   TLS_*AEAD_HASH*

1617   *AEAD* indicates the AEAD algorithm that is used for confidentiality, integrity, and message
1618   authentication. The NIST-approved TLS 1.3 AEAD algorithms comprise a NIST-recommended
1619   block cipher and NIST-recommended AEAD mode.

1620   *HASH* indicates the hashing algorithm that is used as a pseudorandom function during key
1621   derivation.

1622   The following examples illustrate how to interpret TLS 1.3 cipher suite names.
1623   • TLS_AES_256_GCM_SHA384: messages are encrypted and authenticated with AES-
1624   256 in GCM mode, and SHA-384 is used with the HKDF.
1625   • TLS_AES_128_CCM_SHA256: messages are encrypted and authenticated with AES-
1626   128 in CCM mode, and SHA-256 is used with the HKDF.
1627
1628   The negotiation of the key exchange method is handled elsewhere in the TLS handshake.

1629

1630   **Appendix C—Pre-shared Keys**

1631   Pre-shared keys (PSK) are symmetric keys that are already in place prior to the initiation of a
1632   TLS session (e.g., as the result of a manual distribution). The use of PSKs in TLS versions prior
1633   to TLS 1.3 is described in RFC 4279 [29], RFC 5487 [3], and RFC 5489 [4]. Pre-shared keys are
1634   used for session resumption in TLS 1.3. In general, pre-shared keys **should not** be used in TLS
1635   versions prior to TLS 1.3, or for initial session establishment in TLS 1.3. However, the use of
1636   pre-shared keys may be appropriate for some closed environments that have adequate key
1637   management support. For example, they might be appropriate for constrained environments with
1638   limited processing, memory, or power. If PSKs are appropriate and supported, then the following
1639   additional guidelines **shall** be followed.

1640   Recommended pre-shared key (PSK) cipher suites for TLS 1.2 are listed below. Cipher suites for
1641   TLS 1.3 (see Section 3.3.1.2) can all be used with pre-shared keys. Pre-shared keys **shall** be
1642   distributed in a secure manner, such as a secure manual distribution or using a key-establishment
1643   certificate. These cipher suites employ a pre-shared key for entity authentication (for both the
1644   server and the client) and may also use ephemeral Diffie-Hellman (DHE) or ephemeral Elliptic
1645   Curve Diffie-Hellman (ECDHE) algorithms for key establishment. For example, when DHE is
1646   used, the result of the Diffie-Hellman computation is combined with the pre-shared key and
1647   other input to determine the premaster secret.

1648   The pre-shared key **shall** have a minimum security strength of 112 bits. Because these cipher
1649   suites require pre-shared keys, these suites are not generally applicable to common secure web
1650   site applications and are not expected to be widely supported in TLS clients or TLS servers.
1651   NIST suggests that these suites be considered for infrastructure applications, particularly if
1652   frequent authentication of the network entities is required.

1653   Pre-shared key cipher suites may only be used in networks where both the client and server
1654   belong to the same organization. Cipher suites using pre-shared keys **shall not** be used with TLS
1655   1.0 or TLS 1.1, and **shall not** be used when a government client or server communicates with
1656   non-government systems.

1657   TLS 1.2 servers and clients using pre-shared keys may support the following cipher suites:

1658   • TLS_DHE_PSK_WITH_AES_128_GCM_SHA256 (0x00, 0xAA)
1659   • TLS_DHE_PSK_WITH_AES_256_GCM_SHA384 (0x00, 0xAB)
1660   • TLS_ECDHE_PSK_WITH_AES_128_CBC_SHA256 (0xC0, 0x37)
1661   • TLS_ECDHE_PSK_WITH_AES_256_CBC_SHA384 (0xC0, 0x38)
1662   • TLS_DHE_PSK_WITH_AES_128_CCM (0xC0, 0xA6)
1663   • TLS_DHE_PSK_WITH_AES_256_CCM (0xC0, 0xA7)
1664   • TLS_PSK_DHE_WITH_AES_128_CCM_8 (0xC0, 0xAA)
1665   • TLS_PSK_DHE_WITH_AES_256_CCM_8 (0xC0, 0xAB)
1666   • TLS_DHE_PSK_WITH_AES_128_CBC_SHA256 (0x00, 0xB2)
1667   • TLS_DHE_PSK_WITH_AES_256_CBC_SHA384 (0x00, 0xB3)
1668   • TLS_PSK_WITH_AES_128_GCM_SHA256 (0x00, 0xA8)
1669   • TLS_PSK_WITH_AES_256_GCM_SHA384 (0x00, 0xA9)
1670   • TLS_PSK_WITH_AES_128_CCM (0xC0, 0xA4)

1671   • TLS_PSK_WITH_AES_256_CCM (0xC0, 0xA5)

1672   • TLS_PSK_WITH_AES_128_CCM_8 (0xC0, 0xA8)

1673   • TLS_PSK_WITH_AES_256_CCM_8 (0xC0, 0xA9)

1674   • TLS_PSK_WITH_AES_128_CBC_SHA256 (0x00, 0xAE)

1675   • TLS_PSK_WITH_AES_256_CBC_SHA384 (0x00, 0xAF)

1676   • TLS_ECDHE_PSK_WITH_AES_128_CBC_SHA (0xC0, 0x35)

1677   • TLS_ECDHE_PSK_WITH_AES_256_CBC_SHA (0xC0, 0x36)

1678   • TLS_DHE_PSK_WITH_AES_128_CBC_SHA (0x00, 0x90)

1679   • TLS_DHE_PSK_WITH_AES_256_CBC_SHA (0x00, 0x91)

1680   • TLS_PSK_WITH_AES_128_CBC_SHA (0x00, 0x8C)

1681   • TLS_PSK_WITH_AES_256_CBC_SHA (0x00, 0x8D)

1682

1683 **Appendix D—RSA Key Transport**

1684 RSA key transport is a key exchange mechanism where the premaster secret is chosen by the
1685 client, encrypted with the server's public key, and sent to the server. It is available in TLS
1686 versions 1.0 through 1.2, but it is not supported by TLS 1.3. While it is a convenient method for
1687 key exchange when the server's certificate contains an RSA public key, this method has several
1688 drawbacks:

1689   1. The client has sole responsibility for the premaster secret generation. If the client does
1690   not have sufficient entropy to generate the secret, the security of the session will suffer.
1691   2. It does not enable forward secrecy.
1692   3. The padding scheme that TLS uses for this operation has a known vulnerability that
1693   requires TLS implementations to perform attack mitigation.

1694 For these reasons, this guideline does not recommend cipher suites that use RSA key transport
1695 for key exchange (see Section 3.3.1).

1696 Forward secrecy is often a security goal, as it prevents the compromise of long-term keys from
1697 enabling the decryption of sessions. The only way to achieve this property in TLS is to use a key
1698 exchange mechanism that relies on ephemeral parameters (i.e., cipher suites that contain DHE or
1699 ECDHE) as specified in RFC 5246 [24].

1700 RSA key-transport using PKCS #1 v1.5 is vulnerable to vulnerable to Bleichenbacher oracle
1701 attacks. RFC 5246 contains steps to mitigate the attacks by processing incorrectly formatted
1702 messages in a manner indistinguishable from the processing of properly-formatted messages (see
1703 [24], Section 7.4.7.1). The mitigation techniques are not always effective in practice (for
1704 examples, see [13]).

1705 **D.1   Transition Period**

1706 While these guidelines do not recommend cipher suites using RSA key transport, there may be
1707 circumstances in practice where RSA key transport is needed. For example, if an agency uses a
1708 network appliance for regulatory or enterprise security purposes that only functions with these
1709 cipher suites, then these cipher suites may need to be enabled. It is recommended that agencies
1710 transition to a new method to meet their needs as soon as it is practical.

1711 If RSA key transport is needed while a new traffic inspection strategy is being developed, only
1712 RSA key transport cipher suites from the following list may be used. See Section for 3.3.1.1 for
1713 general information on preference order.

1714   • TLS_RSA_WITH_AES_128_CCM (xC0, x9C)
1715   • TLS_RSA_WITH_AES_256_CCM (xC0, x9D)
1716   • TLS_RSA_WITH_AES_128_CCM_8 (xC0, xA0)
1717   • TLS_RSA_WITH_AES_256_CCM_8 (xC0, xA1)
1718   • TLS_RSA_WITH_AES_128_CBC_SHA (x00, x2F)
1719   • TLS_RSA_WITH_AES_256_CBC_SHA (x00, x35)
1720   • TLS_RSA_WITH_AES_128_CBC_SHA256 (x00, 3C)

1721   • TLS_RSA_WITH_AES_256_CBC_SHA256 (x00, 3D)
1722   • TLS_RSA_WITH_AES_128_GCM_SHA256 (x00, x9C)
1723   • TLS_RSA_WITH_AES_256_GCM_SHA384 (x00, x9D)

1724   See transition guidance in SP 800-131A [10] for information on deprecation timelines.

1725 **Appendix E—Future Capabilities**

1726 This section identifies emerging concepts and capabilities that are applicable to TLS. As these
1727 concepts mature, and commercial products are available to support them, these guidelines will be
1728 revised to provide specific recommendations.

1729 ### E.1   U.S. Federal Public Trust PKI

1730 The Identity, Credential, and Access Management (ICAM) Subcommittee of the Federal CIO
1731 Council's Information Security and Identity Management Committee is developing a new public
1732 trust root and issuing CA infrastructure to issue TLS server certificates for federal web services
1733 on the public Internet. The intent is for this new root to be included in all of the commonly used
1734 trust stores so that federal agencies can obtain their TLS server certificates from this PKI rather
1735 than from commercial CAs. The certificate policy for this PKI is being developed at
1736 https://devicepki.idmanagement.gov.

1737 Once this PKI is operational and is included in the commonly used trust stores, federal agencies
1738 should consider obtaining their TLS server certificates from this PKI.

1739 ### E.2   DNS-based Authentication of Named Entities (DANE)

1740 DANE leverages DNS security extensions (DNSSEC) to provide mechanisms for securely
1741 obtaining information about TLS server certificates from the DNS. RFC 6698 [33] specifies a
1742 resource record that may be made available in DNS that includes a certificate (or the public key
1743 of a certificate), along with an indicator of how the certificate is to be used. There are four
1744 options:

1745 1. The DNS record contains an end-entity certificate. In addition to the server public-key
1746   certificate validation as specified in Section 4.5, the client verifies that the TLS server
1747   certificate matches the certificate provided in the DNS records.

1748 2. The DNS record contains a domain-issued end-entity certificate.[35] The client can use the
1749   certificate if it verifies that the TLS server certificate matches the one provided in the
1750   DNS records (i.e., the client forgoes server public-key certificate validation as specified
1751   in Section 4.5).

1752 3. The DNS record contains a CA certificate. In addition to the server public-key certificate
1753   validation as specified in Section 4.5, the client verifies that the certification path for the
1754   TLS server certificate includes the CA certificate provided in the DNS records.

1755 4. The DNS record contains a certificate that is to be used as a trust anchor. The client
1756   validates the TLS server certificate as specified in Section 4.5 using the trust anchor
1757   provided in the DNS records instead of the trust anchors in the client's local trust anchor
1758   store.

---

[35] In this context, a "domain-issued" certificate is one that is issued by the domain name administrator without involving a third-party CA. It corresponds to usage case 3 in Section 2.1.1 of RFC 6698.

1759   In each case, the client verifies the digital signatures on the DNS records in accordance with the
1760   DNSSEC, as described in RFC 4033 [2].

1761   **Appendix F—Determining the Need for TLS 1.0 and 1.1**

1762   Enabling TLS 1.0 or TLS 1.1 when they are not needed may leave systems and users vulnerable
1763   to attacks (such as the BEAST attack and the Klima attack [57]). However, disabling older
1764   versions of TLS when there is a need may deny access to users who are unable to install or
1765   upgrade to a client that is capable of TLS 1.3 or TLS 1.2.

1766   The system administrator must consider the benefits and risks of using TLS 1.0 or TLS 1.1, in
1767   the context of applications supported by the server, and decide whether the benefits of using TLS
1768   1.0 or TLS 1.1 outweigh the risks. This decision should be driven by the service(s) running on
1769   the server and the versions supported by clients accessing the server. Services that do not access
1770   high-value information (such as personally identifiable information or financial data) may
1771   benefit from using TLS 1.0 by increasing accessibility with little increased risk. On the other
1772   hand, services that do access high-value data may increase the likelihood of a breach for
1773   relatively little gain in terms of accessibility. The decision to support TLS 1.0 or TLS 1.1 must
1774   be technically assessed on a case-by-case basis. This is to ensure that supporting older TLS
1775   versions is absolutely necessary and that associated risks and business implications are
1776   understood and accepted.

1777   These guidelines do not give specific recommendations on steps that can be taken to make this
1778   determination. There are tools available (such as the Data Analytics Program [68]) that can
1779   provide information to system administrators that can be used to assess the impact of supporting,
1780   or not supporting, TLS versions prior to TLS 1.2. For example, DAP data on visitor OS and
1781   browser versions can help administrators determine what percentage of visitors to agency
1782   websites cannot negotiate recommended TLS versions by default.

1783   Many products that implement TLS 1.1 also implement TLS 1.2. Because of this, it may be
1784   unnecessary for servers to support TLS 1.1. Administrators can determine whether TLS 1.1 is
1785   needed by assessing whether it must support connections with clients where 1.1 is the highest
1786   TLS version available.

1787   **Appendix G—References**

1788   [1]   AlFardan, N.J., and Paterson, K.G., *Lucky Thirteen: Breaking the TLS and DTLS Record*
1789   *Protocols*, February 2013, http://www.isg.rhul.ac.uk/tls/TLStiming.pdf

1790   [2]   Arends, R., Austein, R., Larson, M., Massey, D., and Rose, S., *DNS Security Introduction*
1791   *and Requirements*, Internet Engineering Task Force (IETF) Request for Comments (RFC) 4033,
1792   March 2005, https://doi.org/10.17487/RFC4033

1793   [3]   Badra, M., *Pre-Shared Key Cipher Suites for TLS with SHA-256/384 and AES Galois*
1794   *Counter Mode*, Internet Engineering Task Force (IETF) Request for Comments (RFC) 5487,
1795   March 2009, https://doi.org/10.17487/RFC5487

1796   [4]   Badra, M., and Hajjeh, I., *ECDHE_PSK Cipher Suites for Transport Layer Security*
1797   *(TLS)*, Internet Engineering Task Force (IETF) Request for Comments (RFC) 5489, March
1798   2009, https://doi.org/10.17487/RFC5489

1799   [5]   Barker, E., *Recommendation for Key Management Part 1: General*, NIST Special
1800   Publication (SP) 800-57 Part 1 Revision 4, National Institute of Standards and Technology,
1801   Gaithersburg, Maryland, January 2016, https://doi.org/10.6028/NIST.SP.800-57pt1r4

1802   [6]   Barker, E., Chen, L., and Moody, D., *Recommendation for Pair-Wise Key-Establishment*
1803   *Schemes Using Integer Factorization Cryptography*, NIST Special Publication (SP) 800-56B
1804   Revision 1, National Institute of Standards and Technology, Gaithersburg, Maryland September
1805   2014, https://doi.org/10.6028/NIST.SP.800-56Br1

1806   [7]   Barker, E., Chen, L., Roginsky, A., Vassilev, A., and Davis, R., *Recommendation for*
1807   *Pair-Wise Key Establishment Schemes Using Discrete Logarithm Cryptography*, Special
1808   Publication (SP) 800-56A Revision 3, National Institute of Standards and Technology,
1809   Gaithersburg, Maryland, April 2018, https://doi.org/10.6028/NIST.SP.800-56Ar3

1810   [8]   Barker, E., and Kelsey, J., *Recommendation for Random Number Generation Using*
1811   *Deterministic Random Bit Generators*, NIST Special Publication (SP) 800-90A Revision 1,
1812   National Institute of Standards and Technology, Gaithersburg, Maryland June 2015,
1813   https://doi.org/10.6028/NIST.SP.800-90Ar1

1814   [9]   Barker, E., and Mouha, N., *Recommendation for the Triple Data Encryption Algorithm*
1815   *(TDEA) Block Cipher*, NIST Special Publication (SP) 800-67 Revision 2, National Institute of
1816   Standards and Technology, Gaithersburg, Maryland, November 2017,
1817   https://doi.org/10.6028/NIST.SP.800-67r2

1818   [10]   Barker, E., and Roginsky, A., *Transitioning the Use of Cryptographic Algorithms and*
1819   *Key Lengths*, NIST Special Publication (SP) 800-131A Revision 2 (draft), National Institute of
1820   Standards and Technology, Gaithersburg, Maryland July 2018,
1821   https://csrc.nist.gov/publications/detail/sp/800-131a/rev-2/draft

1822   [11]   Be'ery, T., and Shulman, A., *A Perfect CRIME? Only TIME Will Tell*, Blackhat Europe,
1823   2013, https://media.blackhat.com/eu-13/briefings/Beery/bh-eu-13-a-perfect-crime-beery-wp.pdf

1824 [12] Bhargavan, K., Lavaud, A.D., Fournet, C., Pironti, A., and Strub, P.Y., *Triple*
1825 *Handshakes and Cookie Cutters: Breaking and Fixing Authentication over TLS*, 2014 IEEE
1826 Symposium on Security and Privacy, May 2014, pp. 98-113, https://doi.org/10.1109/SP.2014.14

1827 [13] Böck, H., Somorovsky, J., and Young, C., *Return Of Bleichenbacher's Oracle Threat*
1828 *(ROBOT)*, Cryptology ePrint Archive, Report 2017/1189, 2017, https://eprint.iacr.org/2017/1189

1829 [14] Bradner, S., *Key words for use in RFCs to Indicate Requirement Levels*, Internet
1830 Engineering Task Force (IETF) Request for Comments (RFC) 2119, March 1997,
1831 https://doi.org/10.17487/RFC2119

1832 [15] CA/Browser Forum, *Baseline Requirements Certificate Policy for the Issuance and*
1833 *Management of Publicly-Trusted Certificates*, https://cabforum.org/baseline-requirements-
1834 documents/

1835 [16] CA/Browser Forum, *Guidelines For The Issuance And Management Of Extended*
1836 *Validation Certificates*, https://cabforum.org/extended-validation

1837 [17] Chernick, C.M., III, C.E., Fanto, M.J., and Rosenthal, R., *Guidelines for the Selection*
1838 *and Use of Transport Layer Security (TLS) Implementations*, NIST Special Publication (SP) 800-
1839 52, National Institute of Standards and Technology, Gaithersburg, Maryland, June 2005,
1840 https://doi.org/10.6028/NIST.SP.800-52

1841 [18] Cooper, D., Santesson, S., Farrell, S., Boeyen, S., Housley, R., and Polk, W., *Internet*
1842 *X.509 Public Key Infrastructure Certificate and Certificate Revocation List (CRL) Profile*,
1843 Internet Engineering Task Force (IETF) Request for Comments (RFC) 5280, 2008,
1844 https://doi.org/10.17487/RFC5280

1845 [19] Dang, Q., *Recommendation for Applications Using Approved Hash Algorithms*, NIST
1846 Special Publication (SP) 800-107 Revision 1, National Institute of Standards and Technology,
1847 Gaithersburg, Maryland August 2012, https://doi.org/10.6028/NIST.SP.800-107r1

1848 [20] Dang, Q., *Recommendation for Existing Application-Specific Key Derivation Functions*,
1849 NIST Special Publication (SP) 800-135 Revision 1, National Institute of Standards and
1850 Technology, Gaithersburg, Maryland, December 2011, https://doi.org/10.6028/NIST.SP.800-
1851 135r1

1852 [21] Dang, Q., and Barker, E., *Recommendation for Key Management, Part 3: Application-*
1853 *Specific Key Management Guidance*, NIST Special Publication (SP) 800-57 Part 3 Revision 1,
1854 National Institute of Standards and Technology, Gaithersburg, Maryland, January 2015,
1855 https://doi.org/10.6028/NIST.SP.800-57pt3r1

1856 [22] Dierks, T., and Allen, C., *The TLS Protocol Version 1.0*, Internet Engineering Task Force
1857 (IETF) Request for Comments (RFC) 2246, January 1999, https://doi.org/10.17487/RFC2246

1858 [23] Dierks, T., and Rescorla, E., *The Transport Layer Security (TLS) Protocol Version 1.1*,
1859 Internet Engineering Task Force (IETF) Request for Comments (RFC) 4346, 2006,
1860 https://doi.org/10.17487/RFC4346

1861   [24]   Dierks, T., and Rescorla, E., *The Transport Layer Security (TLS) Protocol Version 1.2*,
1862   Internet Engineering Task Force (IETF) Request for Comments (RFC) 5246, August 2008,
1863   https://doi.org/10.17487/RFC5246

1864   [25]   Dworkin, M., *Recommendation for Block Cipher Modes of Operation: Galois/Counter*
1865   *Mode (GCM) and GMAC*, NIST Special Publication (SP) 800-38D, National Institute of
1866   Standards and Technology, Gaithersburg, Maryland, November 2007,
1867   https://doi.org/10.6028/NIST.SP.800-38D

1868   [26]   Dworkin, M., *Recommendation for Block Cipher Modes of Operation: Methods and*
1869   *Techniques*, NIST Special Publication (SP) 800-38A, National Institute of Standards and
1870   Technology, Gaithersburg, Maryland, December 2001, https://doi.org/10.6028/NIST.SP.800-
1871   38A

1872   [27]   Dworkin, M., *Recommendation for Block Cipher Modes of Operation: the CCM Mode*
1873   *for Authentication and Confidentiality*, NIST Special Publication (SP) 800-38C, National
1874   Institute of Standards and Technology, Gaithersburg, Maryland, May 2004,
1875   https://doi.org/10.6028/NIST.SP.800-38C

1876   [28]   Eastlake, D., 3rd, *Transport Layer Security (TLS) Extensions: Extension Definitions*,
1877   Internet Engineering Task Force (IETF) Request for Comments (RFC) 6066, January 2011,
1878   https://doi.org/10.17487/RFC6066

1879   [29]   Eronen, P., and Tschofenig, H., *Pre-Shared Key Ciphersuites for Transport Layer*
1880   *Security (TLS)*, Internet Engineering Task Force (IETF) Request for Comments (RFC) 4279,
1881   December 2005, https://doi.org/10.17487/RFC4279

1882   [30]   Federal Public Key Infrastructure Authority, *X.509 Certificate Policy For The U.S.*
1883   *Federal PKI Common Policy Framework*, https://www.idmanagement.gov/fpki/#certificate-
1884   policies

1885   [31]   Freier, A., Karlton, P., and Kocher, P., *The Secure Sockets Layer (SSL) Protocol Version*
1886   *3.0*, Internet Engineering Task Force (IETF) Request for Comments (RFC) 6101, August 2011,
1887   https://doi.org/10.17487/RFC6101

1888   [32]   Gutmann, P., *Encrypt-then-MAC for Transport Layer Security (TLS) and Datagram*
1889   *Transport Layer Security (DTLS)*, Internet Engineering Task Force (IETF) Request for
1890   Comments (RFC) 7366, September 2014, https://doi.org/10.17487/RFC7366

1891   [33]   Hoffman, P., and Schlyter, J., *The DNS-Based Authentication of Named Entities (DANE)*
1892   *Transport Layer Security (TLS) Protocol: TLSA*, Internet Engineering Task Force (IETF)
1893   Request for Comments (RFC) 6698, August 2012, https://doi.org/10.17487/RFC6698

1894   [34]   Joint Task Force Transformation Initiative, *Security and Privacy Controls for Federal*
1895   *Information Systems and Organizations*, NIST Special Publication (SP) 800-53 Revision 4,
1896   National Institute of Standards and Technology, Gaithersburg, Maryland, April 2013,
1897   https://doi.org/10.6028/NIST.SP.800-53r4

1898   [35]   K. Bhargavan, E., Delignat-Lavaud, A., Pironti, A., Langley, A., and Ray, M., *Transport*
1899   *Layer Security (TLS) Session Hash and Extended Master Secret Extension*, Internet Engineering
1900   Task Force (IETF) Request for Comments (RFC) 7627, September 2015,
1901   https://doi.org/10.17487/RFC7627

1902   [36]   Krawczyk, H., and Eronen, P., *HMAC-based Extract-and-Expand Key Derivation*
1903   *Function (HKDF)*, Internet Engineering Task Force (IETF) Request for Comments (RFC) 5869,
1904   May 2010, https://doi.org/10.17487/RFC5869

1905   [37]   Langley, A., *The POODLE bites again*,
1906   https://www.imperialviolet.org/2014/12/08/poodleagain.html

1907   [38]   Langley, A., Modadugu, N., and Moeller, B., *Transport Layer Security (TLS) False Start*,
1908   Internet Engineering Task Force (IETF) Request for Comments (RFC) 7918, August 2016,
1909   https://doi.org/10.17487/RFC7918

1910   [39]   Laurie, B., Langley, A., and Kasper, E., *Certificate Transparency*, Internet Engineering
1911   Task Force (IETF) Request for Comments (RFC) 6962, June 2013,
1912   https://doi.org/10.17487/RFC6962

1913   [40]   McGrew, D., and Bailey, D., *AES-CCM Cipher Suites for Transport Layer Security*
1914   *(TLS)*, Internet Engineering Task Force (IETF) Request for Comments (RFC) 6655, July 2012,
1915   https://doi.org/10.17487/RFC6655

1916   [41]   Moeller, B., and Langley, A., *TLS Fallback Signaling Cipher Suite Value (SCSV) for*
1917   *Preventing Protocol Downgrade Attacks*, Internet Engineering Task Force (IETF) Request for
1918   Comments (RFC) 7507, April 2015, https://doi.org/10.17487/RFC7507

1919   [42]   Möller, B., Duong, T., and Kotowicz, K., *This POODLE Bites: Exploiting The SSL 3.0*
1920   *Fallback*, September 2014, https://www.openssl.org/~bodo/ssl-poodle.pdf

1921   [43]   National Institute of Standards and Technology, *Random Bit Generation*,
1922   https://csrc.nist.gov/Projects/Random-Bit-Generation

1923   [44]   Nir, Y., Josefsson, S., and Pegourie-Gonnard, M., *Elliptic Curve Cryptography (ECC)*
1924   *Cipher Suites for Transport Layer Security (TLS) Versions 1.2 and Earlier*, Internet Engineering
1925   Task Force (IETF) Request for Comments (RFC) 8422, August 2018,
1926   https://doi.org/10.17487/RFC8422

1927   [45]   P. Wouters, E., H. Tschofenig, E., Gilmore, J., Weiler, S., and Kivinen, T., *Using Raw*
1928   *Public Keys in Transport Layer Security (TLS) and Datagram Transport Layer Security (DTLS)*,
1929   Internet Engineering Task Force (IETF) Request for Comments (RFC) 7250, June 2014,
1930   https://doi.org/10.17487/RFC7250

1931   [46]   Paterson, K.G., Ristenpart, T., and Shrimpton, T., *Tag size does matter: attacks and*
1932   *proofs for the TLS record protocol*. Proc. 17th international conference on The Theory and
1933   Application of Cryptology and Information Security, Seoul, South Korea, 2011, Proceedings of
1934   the 17th international conference on The Theory and Application of Cryptology and Information

1935   Security, https://doi.org/10.1007/978-3-642-25385-0

1936   [47]   Pettersen, Y., *The Transport Layer Security (TLS) Multiple Certificate Status Request*
1937   *Extension*, Internet Engineering Task Force (IETF) Request for Comments (RFC) 6961, 2013,
1938   https://doi.org/10.17487/RFC6961

1939   [48]   Polk, T., McKay, K., and Chokhani, S., *Guidelines for the Selection, Configuration, and*
1940   *Use of Transport Layer Security (TLS) Implementations*, NIST Special Publication (SP) 800-52
1941   Revision 1, National Institute of Standards and Technology, Gaithersburg, Maryland, April 2014,
1942   https://doi.org/10.6028/NIST.SP.800-52r1

1943   [49]   Rescorla, E., *TLS Elliptic Curve Cipher Suites with SHA-256/384 and AES Galois*
1944   *Counter Mode (GCM)*, Internet Engineering Task Force (IETF) Request for Comments (RFC)
1945   5289, August 2008, https://doi.org/10.17487/RFC5289

1946   [50]   Rescorla, E., *The Transport Layer Security (TLS) Protocol Version 1.3*, Internet
1947   Engineering Task Force (IETF) Request for Comments (RFC) 8446, August 2018,
1948   https://doi.org/10.17487/RFC8446

1949   [51]   Rescorla, E., Ray, M., Dispensa, S., and Oskov, N., *Transport Layer Security (TLS)*
1950   *Renegotiation Indication Extension*, Internet Engineering Task Force (IETF) Request for
1951   Comments (RFC) 5746, February 2010, https://doi.org/10.17487/RFC5746

1952   [52]   Rizzo, J., and Duong, T., *The CRIME Attack*, EKOparty Security Conference, 2012

1953   [53]   Salowey, J., Choudhury, A., and McGrew, D., *AES Galois Counter Mode (GCM) Cipher*
1954   *Suites for TLS*, Internet Engineering Task Force (IETF) Request for Comments (RFC) 5288,
1955   August 2008, https://doi.org/10.17487/RFC5288

1956   [54]   Salowey, J., Zhou, H., Eronen, P., and Tschofenig, H., *Transport Layer Security (TLS)*
1957   *Session Resumption without Server-Side State*, Internet Engineering Task Force (IETF) Request
1958   for Comments (RFC) 5077, January 2008, https://doi.org/10.17487/RFC5077

1959   [55]   Santesson, S., Myers, M., Ankney, R., Malpani, A., Galperin, S., and Adams, C., *X.509*
1960   *Internet Public Key Infrastructure Online Certificate Status Protocol - OCSP*, Internet
1961   Engineering Task Force (IETF) Request for Comments (RFC) 6960, 2013,
1962   https://doi.org/10.17487/RFC6960

1963   [56]   Seggelmann, R., Tuexen, M., and Williams, M., *Transport Layer Security (TLS) and*
1964   *Datagram Transport Layer Security (DTLS) Heartbeat Extension*, Internet Engineering Task
1965   Force (IETF) Request for Comments (RFC) 6520, February 2012,
1966   https://doi.org/10.17487/RFC6520

1967   [57]   Sheffer, Y., Holz, R., and Saint-Andre, P., *Summarizing Known Attacks on Transport*
1968   *Layer Security (TLS) and Datagram TLS (DTLS)*, Internet Engineering Task Force (IETF)
1969   Request for Comments (RFC) 7457, February 2015, https://doi.org/10.17487/RFC7457

1970   [58]   Springall, D., Durumeric, Z., and Halderman, J.A., *Measuring the Security Harm of TLS*

1971   *Crypto Shortcuts*. Proc. Proceedings of the 2016 Internet Measurement Conference, Santa
1972   Monica, California, USA, 2016, pp. 33-47, https://doi.org/10.1145/2987443.2987480

1973   [59]   The Federal Bridge Certification Authority, *X.509 Certificate Policy For The Federal*
1974   *Bridge Certification Authority (FBCA)*, https://www.idmanagement.gov/fpki/#certificate-policies

1975   [60]   Turan, M.S., Barker, E., Kelsey, J., McKay, K.A., Baish, M.L., and Boyle, M.,
1976   *Recommendation for the Entropy Sources Used for Random Bit Generation*, NIST Special
1977   Publication (SP) 800-90B, National Institute of Standards and Technology, Gaithersburg,
1978   Maryland, January 2018, https://doi.org/10.6028/NIST.SP.800-90B

1979   [61]   U.S. Department of Commerce, *Advanced Encryption Standard*, Federal Information
1980   Processing Standards (FIPS) Publication 197, November 2001,
1981   https://doi.org/10.6028/NIST.FIPS.197

1982   [62]   U.S. Department of Commerce, *Digital Signature Standard (DSS)*, Federal Information
1983   Processing Standards (FIPS) Publication 186-4, July 2013,
1984   https://doi.org/10.6028/NIST.FIPS.186-4

1985   [63]   U.S. Department of Commerce, *The Keyed-Hash Message Authentication Code (HMAC)*,
1986   Federal Information Processing Standards (FIPS) Publication 198-1, July 2008,
1987   https://doi.org/10.6028/NIST.FIPS.198-1

1988   [64]   U.S. Department of Commerce, *Personal Identity Verification (PIV) of Federal*
1989   *Employees and Contractors*, Federal Information Processing Standards (FIPS) Publication 201-
1990   2, August 2013, https://doi.org/10.6028/NIST.FIPS.201-2

1991   [65]   U.S. Department of Commerce, *Secure Hash Standard (SHS)*, Federal Information
1992   Processing Standards (FIPS) Publication 180-4, August 2015,
1993   https://doi.org/10.6028/NIST.FIPS.180-4

1994   [66]   U.S. Department of Commerce, *Security Requirements for Cryptographic Modules*,
1995   Federal Information Processing Standards (FIPS) Publication 140-2, May 2001 (including
1996   Change Notice 2, December 3, 2002), https://doi.org/10.6028/NIST.FIPS.140-2

1997   [67]   U.S. Department of the Treasury, *Public Key Infrastructure (PKI) X.509 Certificate*
1998   *Policy, version 2.9*, March 2017, https://pki.treas.gov/docs/treasury_x509_certificate_policy.pdf

1999   [68]   U.S. General Services Administration, *DAP: Digital Analytics Program*,
2000   https://digital.gov/dap, [accessed September 24, 2018]

2001   [69]   US-CERT/NIST, *CVE-2014-0160*, National Vulnerability Database, 2014,
2002   https://web.nvd.nist.gov/view/vuln/detail?vulnId=CVE-2014-0160

2003   [70]   Yee, P., *Updates to the Internet X.509 Public Key Infrastructure Certificate and*
2004   *Certificate Revocation List (CRL) Profile*, Internet Engineering Task Force (IETF) Request for
2005   Comments (RFC) 6818, January 2013, https://doi.org/10.17487/RFC6818

2006

2007   **Appendix H—Revision History**

2008   **H.1   Original**

2009   The original version of SP 800-52 was published in June 2005 [17]. At the time, only TLS 1.0
2010   was final (TLS 1.1 was still under development). TLS 1.1 became a standard in April 2006, and
2011   TLS 1.2 became a standard in August 2008. SP 800-52 became outdated, and guidance on keys
2012   and cipher suites was incorporated into SP 800-57 Part 3 [21]. In March 2013, SP 800-52 was
2013   withdrawn.

2014   **H.2   Revision 1**

2015   The first revision of SP 800-52 was published in April 2014 [48]. The revision was a new
2016   document that bore little resemblance to the original. At the time, TLS 1.2 was still not prevalent
2017   and the Federal PKI consisted mainly of RSA certificates. Recommendations were made with
2018   this in mind so that federal agencies could follow the guidelines with either existing technology
2019   or technology that was under development. Agencies were advised to develop a plan to migrate
2020   to TLS 1.2.

2021   After revision 1 was posted, the guidance on keys and cipher suites was removed from SP 800-
2022   57 Part 3.

2023   **H.3   Revision 2**

2024   Since revision 1, support for TLS 1.2 and cipher suites using ephemeral key exchanges has
2025   increased, and new attacks have come to light. Revision 2 (this document) requires that TLS 1.2
2026   be supported, and contains several changes to certificate and cipher suite recommendations.

2027   Revision 2 includes recommendations for TLS 1.3. TLS 1.3 offers many improvements over
2028   previous versions of TLS, so revision 2 advises agencies to develop a plan to migrate to TLS 1.3.

2029   Revision 2 also has increased discussion on TLS attacks and guidance on mitigation.

2030   Certificate requirements have also changed in this revision. In particular, status information for
2031   TLS server certificates is required to be made available via the Online Certificate Status
2032   Protocol. This revision of the TLS guidelines relaxes requirements on which signature
2033   algorithms can sign which key types in certificates.

www.ingramcontent.com/pod-product-compliance
Lightning Source LLC
Chambersburg PA
CBHW060205060326
40690CB00018B/4262